DOCTORS AND WHAT THEY DO

harold coy

DOCTORS

and what they do

FRANKLIN WATTS, INC. 575 LEXINGTON AVENUE

NEW YORK 22, N. Y.

contents

DOCTORS AND WHAT THEY DO

1

meet the family doctor

"The doctor is coming!"

These words are a signal for action in any home. Mother tidies up the house and hangs a clean towel in the bathroom. Father shaves and puts on a white shirt. Mother gets the patient into clean pajamas. Frank, the son of the family, is in bed with a cough, a fever, and a runny nose. Just as his mother starts to comb his hair, the doorbell rings.

In walks the doctor with his little black bag. He is a welcome caller. Mother and Father feel worried and helpless, but the doctor knows exactly what to do. He takes Frank's temperature and looks into his mouth.

After a careful examination, he says, "Just as I thought—measles. You'll have to stay in bed a few days, young fellow." Then the doctor sends Father to the drugstore for medicine to loosen Frank's cough. He tells Mother to bathe the patient's eyes and give him plenty of fruit juices and other liquids.

Next day Frank starts breaking out in a red rash. He is a sight, but he doesn't feel as bad as he looks. The doctor calls regularly and shows Frank's parents what to do. They stop worrying. After a few days the rash goes away and Frank is well again.

Nearly all of us had measles while we were growing up. We forgot the measles, but we never forgot the family doctor. He was the first person we ever met who told Mother and Father what to do—and got away with it. They obeyed him, because they wanted us to get well. We too let the doctor do things we wouldn't take from anyone else. He made us open our mouth wide and poked around with a stick. He gave us injections—and, when we were little, a lollipop for being brave. Later he told us we were old enough to be brave without a lollipop.

"See, it doesn't hurt any more than a mosquito bite," he'd say. And it didn't, when the doctor did the sticking. If anyone else had pricked us with a needle, we'd have let out a yell and been ready to fight. But the doctor is a privileged character.

People think of the doctor as one of the smartest and most useful men in town. He guards us from diseases with names other people can't even pronounce. He comes to the rescue of babies so tiny that they must be fed through a medicine dropper and of old people who break their hips and would never walk again without his skillful mending.

Yes, he is a Very Important Person. Almost everyone admires the doctor, and sometimes thinks he would like to *be* a doctor. Here are some stories of what being a doctor is like.

Usually when people talk about a doctor, they mean the family doctor. He treats diseases in all parts of the body, from headaches to athlete's foot. He looks after the health of everyone from baby to grandma.

There are about one hundred and twenty-five thousand of these all-around doctors in the United States, and one of them is Dr. Donald Higgins of Cotuit, a little town on Cape Cod in Massachusetts. Everyone there greets Dr. Higgins with a friendly smile. No wonder. He has been the family doctor for nearly everyone in town for twenty years. And his father was the family doctor for forty years before that!

Dr. Higgins takes care of the grandchildren and great-grandchildren of some of his father's patients. He has delivered nearly a thousand babies.

He is a tall, lean-faced Yankee with glasses. He has thin hair, just turning gray. In his father's time, most doctors wore beards, but Dr. Higgins is clean shaven.

You have to be up early to see the doctor before he leaves on his morning calls. His telephone starts ringing at six o'clock because people know he leaves the house at seven. One morning he let me ride with him and was kind enough to answer questions between calls on patients.

First stop was at a neat, shingled house with blue shutters. A squirrel scampered up a tree. Sea gulls circled the sky. It was early May.

"First nice day we've had on the Cape this spring," someone remarked as the doctor got out.

"Yes, summer's on the way," Dr. Higgins replied. "I took out the first fishhook the other day."

People get fishhooks caught in their skin, even in their face and eyelids, when the fishing season begins. One of the doctor's jobs is to get them out.

Dr. Higgins made his call, then others, until we were eight or ten miles out in the country. It was flat and sandy there with squatty pines and cranberry bogs. People here live in Cape Cod cottages with pitched roofs and little shuttered windows. Some have two windows, some three, and some four.

"A Cape Cod house is supposed to have two windows on each side of the door," explained Dr. Higgins. "But sometimes people start with a half-house or a three-quarters house. Then they add on to it as the family grows."

The doctor makes these "house calls" on people who are too sick or too old to come to his office. Some have a fever or a stomach upset and will be all right after a day or two in bed. Others, with longer-lasting diseases, can be up and around provided the doctor checks up now and then. He examines patients who have had heart attacks and tells them how much they can safely do. He tests a woman with diabetes to find out how much insulin she needs to make use of the sugar in her diet. He gives an elderly man "shots," or injections, of liver extract and Vitamin B12 so that his body can do a better job of making red blood cells. No one knew about this in the time of Dr. Higgins's father. In those days a patient with pernicious anemia, as this disease is called, would have died.

Keeping these people out of serious harm is "preventive medicine," the doctor says. The injections he gives children are preventive medicine too, because they prevent diphtheria, tetanus, whooping cough, poliomyelitis, and smallpox.

At nine o'clock we stopped at Cape Cod Hospital in Hyannis. Dr. Higgins stayed there an hour and saw half a dozen more patients.

Two or three mornings a week, he makes house calls only in an emergency and stays at the hospital from seven-thirty until noon or later. These are the mornings when some of his fellow doctors perform operations. Dr. Higgins gives anesthesia so that the patients can sleep peacefully while the surgeons work.

We went to the children's ward to see two boys and a girl whose tonsils or adenoids had been removed the day before.

The boys were ready to go home. Six-year-old Mary had to have a gauze pack taken out of her nose. Dr. Higgins told her, "What I have to do is cut the string on it. So you let me know if I pull too hard.

It will be uncomfortable but it won't hurt too much."

Mary whimpered just a little as the doctor held the pack with one hand and cut with the other. He worked speedily and gently.

"Hold right still. You know, I think it would be better if you would lie down. Hold still now." Snip went the scissors. "Blow your nose if you want to." She blew. "Now open your mouth big and I am going to haul that out. Open up big. Say ah!" And out came the pack.

Dr. Higgins called Mary's mother by telephone. "I am going to give her some penicillin to take care of any infection. I'll call the hospital back around two or three this afternoon and if she is O.K., with no bleeding, she can leave tomorrow. She was an awfully nice little girl. It was a nasty thing but she was a good girl about it."

Leaving the hospital, we talked about children as patients.

"Some children make a big fuss no matter what you do," said Dr. Higgins. "But most of them are very reasonable if you explain ahead of time that it is going to hurt. The main thing is to be honest. If you tell a child it isn't going to hurt, and it does, he'll never trust you again. It's better to explain what you have to do and then do it quickly. It may hurt for a moment, but they don't hold it against you."

We climbed into the doctor's fast, sleek convertible. On the way home, between more house calls, Dr. Higgins told how things were when his father was a doctor.

"A horse and buggy was the only way to get around when Dad began practicing medicine. He kept three or four horses so he could change between trips. About 1900 he got a Stanley Steamer. It was the first automobile on Cape Cod and worked by steam instead of gasoline. I can still remember it. You would have to build a charcoal fire to get it going. Later Dad rode a motorcycle with a chain drive. One day the chain came off, the motorcycle stopped, and Dad went over the handlebars and landed on his hands. It took the skin off both palms."

The telephone was just coming in. Most people in the country had no phones. They sent a hired man or their oldest boy into town to get the doctor. Day or night, the doctor had to start out on the long trip.

Dr. Higgins's father performed many an operation on the kitchen table by the light of a kerosene lamp. Sometimes a farmer's appendix was ready to burst and make trouble. The doctor put the patient to sleep with ether, then showed the farmer's wife how to keep on giving it, drop by drop, while he took the appendix out. Before starting, he was careful to scrub his hands and boil his instruments. This was a new-fangled idea then, but it kept germs out of the wound and made the operation a success.

Dr. Higgins's father was a doctor for twenty-five

years before there was a hospital on Cape Cod. Doctors were just beginning to learn about X-rays. They had only a few of the present tests for examining blood and specimens for signs of disease.

The older Dr. Higgins spent much of his time treating diphtheria, typhoid fever, pneumonia, and other germ diseases. His son has never seen a case of diphtheria. Typhoid fever has almost disappeared since milk and drinking water were made safe.

"Pneumonia was pretty serious even when I started in practice," said Dr. Higgins. "But now, with drugs like penicillin, we see it much more rarely, and when we do, it is less serious."

Sometimes people speak of the "good old days." But they were not good for babies. Many a mother lost two or three babies from "summer complaint." It came from spoiled food. Today people have better refrigerators and healthier babies.

Dr. Higgins sees far fewer cases of tuberculosis than his father did. When he does see them, he knows how to stop the progress of the disease more quickly. As a result, the illness is not so likely to spread to other people. Part of the county tuberculosis sanitarium is being changed into a hospital for old people with hardened arteries or ailing joints. People live longer nowadays. Dr. Higgins's patients live to be seventy years old, on the average. In his father's time, the average life lasted fifty or fifty-five years. Dr. Higgins has a son who is studying to be a doctor.

Perhaps he will see as many changes as his grandfather and his father did.

"I carry around a lot of supplies, but they come
in handy," said Dr. Higgins, pointing to the back of
the car. On the seat and floor were:

A storm coat and hat. It can rain
almost any time in New England.

Several medical journals the doctor
reads when he stops for car repairs.
To keep up with what is happening,
he has to make every minute count.
He has a car radio so he can listen
to the news while he drives.

A small electrocardiograph machine to carry
to a patient's bedside. This is
an instrument he uses to examine
the action of the heart.

A small tank of oxygen under pressure
—to help patients who are struggling
for breath. "I am quite sure that
little tank has saved one man's life
twice and some others once," said
Dr. Higgins.

Last but not least, the doctor's
bag.

When we reached the house, Dr. Higgins opened
his bag. Inside were examining instruments, a blood-

pressure apparatus, adhesive tape and gauze, pain-killing drugs and other drugs, local anesthesia, syringes, clamps to stop the flow of blood, needles to put in stitches and scissors to take them out, dry penicillin, and distilled water for mixing it. The doctor doesn't forget anything. He has hair clippers he uses before putting on an adhesive bandage so the hair won't pull when the bandage comes off. And he has a life-saving tube with which he can make an airway into the windpipe in case a man is choking on a fish bone.

It was one o'clock. Dr. Higgins has his office at home, and patients were arriving. Mrs. Higgins had a glass of milk and a sandwich ready for her husband. He was through with his lunch in a few minutes. Then he opened the door into the waiting room and asked, "Who's first?"

It was the beginning of a long afternoon. Dr. Higgins would see a dozen or more patients with backaches, headaches, stomach-aches, sniffles, bruises, and sprains. Most of these office visits are for minor complaints, but Dr. Higgins looks at everyone carefully, because sometimes the aches and pains are early signs of something more serious.

Dr. and Mrs. Higgins have many friends who invite them out to dinner. All the doctor can ever say is, "I'll come if I can." He never knows when he will have to hurry away because a baby is arriving or someone has been hurt in an automobile accident.

Sometimes he excuses himself after twenty or thirty minutes to return to his office, because on two evenings a week he sees patients from seven until nine o'clock. Then maybe he goes out on two or three more house calls.

After that it would be nice to sleep until six in the morning. Often, though, someone gets sick during the night. Then the telephone wakes up the doctor, and he may have to dress, pack up his bag, and go out on a night call.

Many people come to Cape Cod for summer vacations. While others are having fun, Dr. Higgins carries a double load. He looks after the health of the year-round people and the summer people too.

Mrs. Higgins, always cheerful and friendly, answers the phone when the doctor is away, and takes messages. She also sends out the doctor's bills.

Dr. Higgins is never idle for a moment, but when he is with a patient he never acts busy. He always has time to listen and say a comforting word. This means a lot to sick people. One sick old man couldn't get to the barber shop. His hair grew long and scraggly over his ears until he felt sicker than he was. Dr. Higgins said, "I can take care of that in two seconds." He borrowed a pair of electric clippers from the barber down the street. With these and his scissors he gave the man a fine treatment.

A woman had cancer that had gone too far to be cured. People said, "There is nothing the doctor can do." But there was. He stopped by every day and chatted with her about recipes and the way she fixed her hair and nails. He checked on how much medicine she needed to relieve the pain.

"There is a lot you can do not to mind being sick so much," Dr. Higgins told his patient.

The sick woman's last days were more agreeable than you might think possible. "He is the nicest doctor I ever knew," she told her daughter.

Recently this daughter set aside a sum of money in memory of her mother. She knew that Dr. Higgins sees many patients who are too poor to buy braces, eyeglasses, and expensive medicines. So she asked the doctor to use the money as he sees fit and help them get the things they need. Others in the town are joining in with their gifts. So now there is a tidy little fund in this corner of Cape Cod. It helps the doctor help people get well—or at least not mind being sick so much.

2

how doctors get their facts

"Doctor, I have a stomach-ache."

"Where does it hurt you?"

One patient may point to his abdomen, another to his chest. Lots of people call any part of the trunk, from the neck to the legs, their stomach. But a doctor has to be more exact. He wants to know just where the pain is and much else too.

"Where did the pain start? Was it in the daytime or at night? Did it wake you up? What did you have to eat before going to bed? Does the pain get worse after you eat, or feel better? Does it come and go? Is it a sharp or dull pain? Does it stay in one place or does it shoot out, and where? Is it getting better or does it stay about the same? How bad is the pain? Does it double you up? Have you taken anything for it? Do you have any other pains with it—headache, pains in your legs or arms?"

The doctor fires questions like a district attorney. If he is the regular family doctor, he already has a record of the past illnesses of the patient and his family. He calls this a "medical history." It shows whether the patient has ever had anything wrong with his eyes, nose, ears, mouth, throat, lungs, heart, digestive tract, kidneys, arms and legs, and nervous system. What does he do at work and play? What are his daily habits?

A "stomach-ache" can mean almost anything. Many times it's caused by something the patient ate and will soon be over. All the patient needs is medicine to relieve the discomfort. But it *could* mean an ulcer, or appendicitis, or kidney stones. So, if the doctor is in doubt, he asks plenty of questions.

He's a detective as well as a district attorney. He puts a thermometer into the patient's mouth. He looks at his watch and counts the pulse. He feels the abdomen for tender or swollen spots and muscles with kinks in them. He searches for the spleen and the edge of the liver. He looks at the shape of the chest and the color of the skin.

A doctor's eyes, ears, and fingers are among his best tools. He lays a finger on the chest, taps it with a finger of the other hand, holds his ear close, and listens. Just as you tell by thumping a watermelon whether it is green or ripe and juicy, so the doctor finds out what it is like inside the chest. If he taps over air, it sounds like a drum. If he taps over liquid, the sound is dull or flat. In this way, the doctor can

size up the condition of the lungs and get an idea of
how big the heart is.

Of course another way the doctor listens is with
his stethoscope. The earpieces, rubber tube, and chest
piece let him study the heartbeat and the passage of
air into the lungs. He moves the instrument from
place to place and asks the patient to cough or
breathe deep, or count up to ten.

"Hey, the pain's not up there, it's in my stomach,"
the patient may say. But the doctor knows what he
is doing. Sometimes the pain is one place and the
real trouble somewhere else. So the doctor looks and
listens and taps, first one place, then another. He is
a detective with a list of those who *might* have com-
mitted the crime. Most of the suspects have a good
alibi, but finally the finger of guilt points to one of
them who may not have seemed like the culprit at all.

A doctor has to keep his ears and eyes open and
miss nothing. He hears more through his stethoscope
than just a heart beating. "Lubb, dupp, lubb, dupp,"
is the ordinary sound he hears. Sometimes he may
hear what sounds like a cat purring or lapping milk
out of a saucer. Some of these special sounds may be
clues to disease; others are unimportant and will go
away.

Healthy breathing sounds like a soft breeze in the
woods. But if the lungs are stopped up and little
bubbles are bursting with every breath, then what

the doctor hears resembles the crackling of a fire in the brush. Air forcing its way through sticky passages sounds like salt tossed into the fire. A patient who is breathing hard from asthma feels miserable but sounds almost like a music box.

A doctor sizes up his patient's posture, body build, and way of walking. He notices the tiniest details. A rash doesn't mean much to most people, but a doctor asks himself: Is it in one place or in patches? Are the eruptions separate or do they run together? Do they form a shape like a spiral, a ring, a rainbow, a necklace, a girdle? Are they spotty or bumpy, solid or full of liquid, black, red, or brown? There are many kinds of rashes, and the doctor has to know the details of each.

He even learns to use his nose. Some people owe their lives to the doctor's educated sense of smell. If a man collapses on the street and has an odor on his breath, most people think he is drunk. They wait for a policeman to take him to jail. But if a doctor passes by and takes a sniff, he may say, "That's not alcohol. It's acetone. This man is in a diabetic coma. Call an ambulance." At the hospital, injections of insulin can save the man's life.

It is easy to see that a doctor develops his natural powers of observation far more than do most people. But this is not enough. He needs to see deeper than his eyes will let him. Suppose he wants to look far up into your nose. He straps on a head mirror,

makes the room half dark, and turns on a lamp near
your head. The beams of light strike the mirror, and
the reflection lights up your nose. The doctor looks
inside with a speculum. It has handles like a pair of
pliers, with curved blades at the end to hold the
nostril open. When the doctor wants to look down
into the throat, he uses a wooden tongue depressor
and a mirror with a long handle. He can look at a
sore eardrum with an instrument called the otoscope.

The doctor can even see through to the back of
the eyes. To do this he uses an ophthalmoscope and
lights up the retina. You might think the only reason
for examining the eyes is to see whether the patient
needs glasses. Actually the retina is the only place
in the body where the doctor can look directly at
the small blood vessels and see what shape they are
in. Early signs of diseases in other parts of the body
often show up here.

Doctors believe it is a good idea to have regular
physical examinations without waiting until you are
sick. Taking the blood pressure is part of most examinations. The doctor wraps a cloth cuff around
your arm. Inside is a rubber bag, and the doctor
pumps it full of air. Tighter and tighter gets the bag,
and up goes the mercury column in a registering
instrument. Meanwhile the doctor listens with his
stethoscope at the bend of your elbow. He hears
blood rushing through the arteries—and then silence.
The pulse at your wrist grows still. This means that

no more blood can pass the tight band. Now the doctor lets out a little air until the circulation returns. He reads the mercury column. This is your blood pressure at the full force of the heart's pumping action. Then the doctor lets out more air until the beats grow feeble—and this is the lower pressure where the heart is filling up with blood.

The busy heart muscle generates tiny electric currents. Sometimes the doctor wants to know about these too. This is where the electrocardiograph comes in. The doctor fastens electrodes to the patient's arms, legs, and chest. Wires carry the electric impulses to moving photographic film, or to paper, where they are traced as jiggly lines. The pattern of the lines tells a doctor a lot about the way the heart is working.

A wall of flesh stands between the doctor and this living heart, but he can see through the wall with the help of an X-ray picture. Each shadow on the X-ray plate tells the doctor something about the condition of the inner organs. He can also look at the shadows in motion. To do this he passes X-rays through the patient's body and watches the shadows on a glowing fluorescent screen.

The doctor's microscope lets him count the very cells of your blood. The doctor or his nurse takes a little blood from the tip of your finger or the lobe of your ear. Parts of it are mixed with other liquids. A drop from one batch goes into a glass counting chamber and spreads over a surface that is ruled off into little squares. The red blood cells show up under the microscope. The doctor or nurse counts the cells in several squares, then multiplies to get your "hemoglobin," or "red-cell count." This is the number of red cells in a cubic millimeter of blood. A millimeter is only about one twenty-fifth of an inch, but a cube of this size may have four and a half or five million red cells, all busy carrying oxygen throughout the body. People with anemia have fewer red cells than this, but people who live high in the mountains, or have trouble with their breathing, may have more of these oxygen-bearing cells.

Another batch of blood in solution gives the "white-cell count." The white blood cells multiply in order to resist invading germs. If a patient complains of a pain in his abdomen and the doctor finds twice as many white cells as usual, he suspects appendicitis.

If your doctor knows you are curious about science, he may show you how he does a hemoglobin test and measures the iron in a blood sample. Perhaps he mixes a little blood with hydrochloric acid in a measuring tube, then adds water until it matches the shade of red in a piece of colored glass. Some doctors use a photoelectric eye to match the colors.

Various chemical tests reveal the contents of the blood and other body fluids. One of the most common is the Benedict sugar test. The doctor pours a small amount of blue fluid into a tube and adds a few drops from a specimen of urine. If the mixture stays blue, it means no sugar is present. If it turns yellow or brick red, there is probably sugar, and the doctor makes further tests for possible diabetes.

A doctor doesn't jump to conclusions from just one clue any more than a detective takes it for granted that a suspect is guilty because he was near the scene of the crime or once had a quarrel with the victim. A doctor must have enough clues to prove his case or he may "give the right treatment for the wrong disease." Suppose three-year-old Barbara has a tight feeling in her chest, a dry cough, and wheezy breathing. It looks like a little bronchitis that will go away with rest in bed and proper diet. But sometimes these same symptoms mark the beginning of whooping cough or pneumonia. The doctor examines Barbara carefully and rules out these possibilities. But other signs puzzle him, so he decides to take X-rays of Barbara's chest. Here he finds evidence that something is stuck in the air passages of the lungs.

"She must have swallowed something she was playing with, and it went down her windpipe," says the doctor. He takes Barbara to the hospital and, while she is under anesthesia, he or another doctor probes into the air passage with an instrument called the bronchoscope. Out comes a safety pin! It might have been a button, a pebble, a piece of crayon, a penny, a nickel, or even a quarter. Many hospitals keep a box with a collection of things young children have swallowed. The objects are in the box instead of in the children because some doctors took the trouble to make careful diagnoses.

Diagnosis means finding what the real trouble is, so that the doctor can do something about it. A doctor gathers many clues. Some lead in the wrong direction, and he discards them. Others are more convincing, but the doctor checks one fact against another, many times, before he makes up his mind. You can see how easy it would be for a person who is not a doctor to overlook bits of evidence or go astray on a false clue.

In making a diagnosis, a doctor has many aids. He draws on his long experience and looks into big books where hundreds of diseases are described. He has the help of X-ray and laboratory equipment— some in his own office and a lot more he can make use of in other places. Much of today's equipment is too big and expensive even for a doctor with a big office and a nurse and a technician to help him. So it is kept in a hospital or a clinic where many doctors can share it. This marvelous equipment is the key to secrets that no doctor of your grandfather's time could ever hope to know.

Yet even today a doctor often finds himself at the bedside of someone who is sick, far out in the country, or in the middle of the night, or at the height of a blizzard. Then his only tools, for the moment, are those in his bag and the back seat of his car, plus his eyes, ears, and fingers. A doctor's keen senses and his trained mind are his most precious gift—something he always has with him.

3

new weapons doctors use

The circus tent at Hartford, Connecticut, was crowded with children and their parents. One exciting act followed another—trapeze artists in daring feats, bareback riders, elephants on parade, snarling lions and leopards leaping through hoops at the crack of the ringmaster's whip. There were plenty of laughs too. The clowns saw to that.

Suddenly something happened that was not on the program. Cries of "Fire! Fire!" rang out. Flames shot up at one end of the big canvas top and spread rapidly. Fear took hold of the audience. People pushed and struggled up the aisles to get out. Some perished in the towering flames. Ambulances with wailing sirens carried eighty-seven of the most badly burned, who were still alive, to Hartford Hospital.

This happened in 1944. If it had happened in 1934 or 1924, fully half of those eighty-seven persons might have died. As it was, eighty-four, or all but three, got well. Doctors had to battle for weeks to save them, but they had powerful new weapons with which to fight.

One of these weapons was the blood bank. Some of the circus-fire victims received fifteen or twenty pints of blood or of plasma, the fluid part of blood. These transfusions were real lifesavers. In a bad burn, lots of fluid seeps out of the capillaries—the smallest vessels of the circulatory system. The blood left behind gets sticky and sluggish. It doesn't carry enough oxygen to the liver, kidneys, heart, and brain. There must be transfusions to make up for the lost liquid and keep the blood circulating.

Another weapon was new knowledge of body chemistry. The water balance is easily upset in serious injuries—and two-thirds of the body is made up of water. The hospital doctors looked after that too. The water they gave to patients had carefully measured amounts of salt and other minerals to bring the body fluids back into balance. Any patient who was too sick to drink received these solutions through a vein.

Food was still another weapon. To rebuild tissue destroyed by fire takes huge amounts of protein such as is found in lean meats, fish, milk, and eggs. The patients needed several times as much as they were used to eating at a time when they felt anything but hungry. The doctors coaxed them to eat protein-rich foods. Nurses tempted them with eggnogs and glasses of cream. Finally, the patients could hold no more,

and still it was not enough. So the doctors ordered
more blood transfusions. They knew that blood contains a good deal of protein.

Of course there was much more to the treatment
—drugs to ease pain, dressings for the wounds, oxygen when needed, and skin grafts to repair the damage. And there were shots of penicillin to keep down
infection. In the old days a patient would sometimes
seem to be getting well, but then his wound would
become infected with deadly germs. It was the beginning of blood poisoning, often more dangerous
than the burn itself. No one who was burned at the
circus died that way at Hartford Hospital. The
reason was penicillin, the new "wonder drug."

Since then, doctors have saved millions of lives and
prevented untold suffering with penicillin. They use
it every day to fight infections in every part of the
body caused by many different disease germs. A patient with one of the common types of pneumonia
gets penicillin and feels better the next day. Without
it he would be lucky to get well in two weeks.

Probably your father can remember children who
came back to school with scars in front of one or
both ears from a mastoid operation. Today this operation is rare, for penicillin usually stops ear infections in time.

When penicillin gets into the blood stream, it kills
certain germs or slows their growth enough to let
the body fight off the invaders. It is the number-one

antibiotic in the doctor's bag. "Antibiotic" means something that acts against life; in this case, against germ life. There were antibiotics in nature long before doctors discovered them. Actually antibiotics are substances that one form of microscopic life produces for defense against another. The ones doctors look for are those that harm disease germs without harming people.

Penicillin comes from a fungus mold. Other antibiotics, even newer, are produced by microbes that live in the soil. Some of these act against so many different kinds of germs that they are called "broad-spectrum" antibiotics. They are useful in many diseases, including some, such as whooping cough and typhoid fever, that penicillin doesn't seem to help. An antibiotic called streptomycin helps tuberculosis patients get well faster, provided they have proper rest in bed and other treatment.

Drugs made from chemicals supply doctors with other valuable weapons. They use the sulfa drugs to treat many diseases, sometimes in combination with penicillin or other drugs. Thousands of children who once would have died of meningitis owe their lives to the sulfas. The remarkable nitrofuran drugs come from corn cobs and oat hulls. The doctor may use one of these drugs when he dresses your infected toe. Another clears up certain kidney and bladder infections.

Do doctors have a wonder drug to cure colds? No, and it's a mistake to beg the doctor for a shot of penicillin for every case of sniffles. Ask your doctor and he will tell you that penicillin won't cure a cold. It should be used only when the doctor thinks the cold might be complicated by a bacterial infection.

Penicillin is for shooting bears, not rabbits. If it is used for every minor ailment, some people become allergic to it after a while, and the germs can grow resistant to it.

Doctors like to tell a story about a man with a cold. He said to his doctor, "Give me a shot of penicillin so I can get well in a hurry and go about my business."

The doctor replied: "My advice is to stay in bed for a couple of days. Your cold will soon be over. Meanwhile, I can help you feel more comfortable."

"But I want you to cure me," insisted the man.

"All right, take off your shoes, go outdoors, and run around in the snow for half an hour."

"But I'll catch pneumonia, doctor!"

"Well, pneumonia we can cure."

Of course the doctor knew that pneumonia is really no laughing matter. What he meant was that most pneumonia is caused by germs called bacteria that antibiotics can fight. Colds start from a virus infection. Viruses are the smallest germs of all—too

tiny to be seen through an ordinary microscope—
and only a few of the larger viruses are hurt by any
antibiotics that doctors know about yet.

Nevertheless, doctors have other weapons against
some of the viruses. For a long time they have known
how to head off the virus of smallpox with vaccina-
tion. They have a new vaccine to use against polio.
Now they are working hard to perfect a vaccine
against influenza.

Measles is another virus disease. Usually it is a mild
illness, but it can be tough on babies or on children
who are in a run-down condition. So if young children are exposed to measles, the doctor may give an
injection of GG as protection against a bad case of
the disease. GG is short for gamma globulin, one of
the substances contained in blood collected at the
blood bank. How can GG help with measles? Well,
most of the people who donate blood had measles
when they were children. At that time they developed antibodies against the virus. When they went
to the blood bank, antibodies were still in their blood,
protecting them from measles. They passed on some
of this protection with their gift of blood.

The doctor gives you "shots" so that you will
produce your own antibodies against the viruses and
bacteria that cause various diseases. Usually these
"shots" are made from dead or weakened germs or
their products. Smallpox vaccine contains the viruses
of a milder disease called cowpox. Luckily, the anti-

bodies you make against cowpox work against smallpox too.

Some of the doctor's most valuable weapons are
not for use against germs at all. He has new and better drugs to relieve hay fever, help ulcers heal,
strengthen a faltering heart, and ward off the misery
of seasickness.

Perhaps the most amazing drugs of all are manu-
factured in your own body. These are the hormones.
They are produced by various glands and pass into
the blood stream, where they act as chemical mes-
sengers to other parts of the body. Tiny amounts of
hormones control happenings of great importance
such as growing up into manhood and womanhood.
They have a lot to do with our alertness and vigor
and the speed at which we live. When we are angry
or frightened or face any emergency, the hormones
are in there fighting.

Many hormones are now made outside the body,
either from animal glands or by chemical means.
Probably the most talked about hormone is cortisone.
With it, doctors relieve attacks of asthma and the
painful, swollen joints of rheumatic arthritis. But
they use cortisone with great care, for it is a powerful drug and can make the face puffy and do other
harm if it is not watched closely. Another hormone,
hydrocortisone, is safer, since it can be used as an
ointment or injected into a swollen joint without
acting on the whole system. Doctors use this hor-

mone for many rashes and itches, including poison ivy.

Another hormone, thyroxin, helps people with a lazy thyroid gland get back their pep and zest for life. Other people take regular injections of insulin, a hormone necessary for making use of the sugar in the diet. Their own bodies do not produce enough insulin, but if they receive it from outside and follow the doctor's advice about diet and hygiene, they get along well. Before insulin was discovered, young people with diabetes died early, but now they can live perfectly normal lives and engage in all kinds of sports.

Finally we reach the borderline between drugs and food. Vitamins, for example, are called drugs if you buy them at a drugstore and food if you get them in a well-balanced diet. Anyway, they are a "must" in good nutrition. And nutrition is a science doctors study carefully in order to treat disease and keep people healthy. Lack of Vitamin C causes scurvy, a disease in which the gums grow spongy and blood vessels break easily. Sailors on long voyages often died of scurvy before ship captains learned to carry citrus fruits along. Doctors know that Vitamin D is necessary to prevent rickets. Older doctors can remember how some children grew up bow-legged in the days before they got Vitamin D from fish-liver oil and irradiated foods.

These extreme conditions are rare in the United States now, thanks to what doctors have taught us about nutrition. But we still don't stay as healthy as we might if we listened to the doctor more.

Too many people skip breakfast and hurry off to work or school without energy foods to carry them through the morning.

Lonely old people start living on toast and tea because it's too much trouble to fix a full meal just for themselves. As a result, they feel older than they really need to.

And doctors find that young people from ten years old on through the teens are often the worst nourished of all. They are growing so fast that they need as much of certain food substances as a man doing heavy work—sometimes more. They need calcium for bone building and iron for red blood. They need foods rich in protein for muscles and nerves and a sure supply of antibodies and hormones. And they need the vitamins that spark the body's chemistry in countless ways.

Ask a doctor what happens when teen-agers fill up on candy, soda pop, and a hot dog, and he will say, "Too many carbohydrates—sugars and starches. These foods supply quick energy, but too much of them spoils the appetite for body-building foods with necessary vitamins, minerals, proteins, and fats. Then young people fall behind in their growth or complain of poor teeth or poor complexion. They tire easily and don't have as much fun as they could if they paid attention to good nutrition."

Doctors often talk about "the Basic Seven food groups" and remind us that we need foods from each group every day:

> Dark green, leafy, and deep yellow vegetables.
> Citrus fruits, tomatoes, raw cabbage.
> Potatoes and other vegetables and fruit.
> Milk, cheese, ice cream.
> Meat, poultry, fish, eggs, dried beans and
>   peas, nuts.
> Bread and cereals—whole grain or enriched
>   and restored.
> Butter or fortified margarine.

Doctors advise mothers about the baby's formula and they advise people of all ages about their diet. Girls who are beginning to date want to look attractive and may think they need to take off weight. But it is a mistake to go on a strict diet without asking the doctor. It is too easy to miss out on some necessary vitamin or mineral. Besides, a girl may want to be slimmer than it is healthy for her to be. The doctor will know, and if she really needs to reduce, he can prescribe a safe diet.

Lots of people in middle life get too fat. One of the family doctor's big jobs is to help these people keep their weight down, because if they stay fat they are more liable to develop high blood pressure, hard-

ening of the arteries, diabetes, and other diseases than
people of normal weight. But, like people of any age,
they need the doctor as a guide when they reduce.

In fact, the family doctor is a good lifetime guide.
In the early years, he helps us realize the full possibilities of health and happiness. As we grow older, he
attends to our aches and pains and keeps us well. He
teaches us to dodge the diseases of later life as long as
we can, and after that he teaches us how to live with
them more comfortably.

The doctor commands many weapons for our protection—powerful new drugs and time-tried older
remedies, blood and plasma, minerals, vitamins, and
hormones. But of course his most important weapon
is his deep understanding of the human body and
how it works, and what he can safely do to help it
work better. Doctors are learning more about human
life processes all the time. And what they are finding
out is more than enough to make us marvel as Shake-
speare did long ago when he wrote: "What a piece
of work is man! How noble in reason! How infinite
in faculties! In form and moving how express and
admirable."

4

all kinds of doctors

So far we have talked mostly about family doctors, who look after the health of the whole family and treat many kinds of disease. Sometimes a doctor decides he wants to do some special kind of work all the time. Perhaps he becomes a children's doctor, or an expert on the heart or the eyes, or a surgeon known for his skill in certain operations. Doctors like these are specialists.

Some people say, "When I'm sick, I want to go to a specialist, because he knows more." Others say, "There are too many specialists. What we need are more family doctors." Actually it is a good thing that there are both kinds. We need a steady family doctor who knows us from long experience. And sometimes we need a specialist for some special problem. If so, the family doctor knows where to find a good one. In fact, he sometimes tells a family, "This is an unusual case, and I'd like to call in a specialist and consult with him." It's often a very good idea for two doctors to put their heads together. Medical knowledge has become so vast that the smartest doctor in the world can't know everything about everything.

In the country and in smaller places, family doctors usually look after mothers-to-be and deliver their babies. They do this in cities too, but there are doctors called obstetricians who specialize in this kind of work. The obstetrician is a good specialist to start with because he takes care of people even before they are born.

Let's suppose that Anne Rogers is a young married woman who is expecting her first baby. She makes an appointment to visit the obstetrician. How many things she needs to know!

The obstetrician, with the help of his nurse, makes an examination. Part of it is like any physical checkup. In addition, the obstetrician looks for the body changes that take place when a woman is about to become a mother and measures the bones of the pelvis.

"You are in fine health, Mrs. Rogers, and I am sure you are going to have your baby without any difficulty. Remember, motherhood is one of the most natural things in the world," he says.

Mrs. Rogers returns every month for several months, then every two weeks, and finally every week. She learns what to wear and what to eat and how much to rest.

"I've always been fond of swimming and outdoor

activities. I suppose I'll have to give that up," she says with a sigh on one of her early visits.

"No, you can continue for quite a while. Just don't go in for high-diving. And quit before you're tired," replies the obstetrician.

The patient steps on the scales to be weighed every time she visits the doctor's office. He discusses her diet. A friend has told her, "Now you must eat for two." The obstetrician explains that this is a half-truth, almost worse than an untruth.

"Some women fill up on jelly, cookies, and chocolate malts. Then they wonder why they don't get back their nice figures after the baby comes." He writes out a diet with only a few more calories than usual but plenty of extra vitamins and minerals—especially the calcium found in milk. "These are the foods your baby needs," says the obstetrician.

He tells Mrs. Rogers to call him if she notices any symptoms she can't understand, but he watches her so carefully that trouble never comes. It gives her confidence to see that her doctor knows his work so well. She is sure everything is going to be all right.

The obstetrician can usually tell within a week or two when the baby is due. Long ahead of time he helps Mrs. Rogers arrange for her stay at the hospital. During the last months he can hear the baby's heart beating. He usually hears just one heart. If he heard two, he would tell her to get ready for twins.

Finally the time draws near. Mrs. Rogers has her

suitcase packed for the trip to the hospital. Her husband is more nervous than she is. When the first signs appear that the baby is on the way, he bundles his wife into the car and drives toward the hospital at top speed. He is so excited about the baby's coming that he doesn't see a red light and has to explain to the policeman. Fortunately, the policeman is excited about babies too and waves him on. There is probably no need for such hurry. It may be many hours yet before the baby is born.

During the waiting period, Mr. Rogers stays in the father's room at the hospital and paces the floor, anxious for news. The obstetrician checks up on the baby's progress every little while. He never goes far away because the nurse may call him at any time. He has a cot in the hospital on which to catch half an hour's sleep now and then. Day or night, babies come when they get ready. Sometimes an obstetrician is up several nights in a row. He must learn to nap when he can.

Mrs. Rogers's obstetrician gives her medicines so she will feel more comfortable, but he doesn't give enough to hurt the baby. She knows from what the doctor has said that the more she puts her mind at rest the less pain she will feel. The doctor would like her to stay at least partly awake so she can follow instructions and help in the delivery.

The great moment arrives. Everything goes according to plan in the delivery room.

"It's a boy!" says the obstetrician. The mother is drowsy but she hears the words and thinks, "How happy his father will be!" If it had been a girl, she would have had the same thought.

The first thing the baby does is cry. This is his way of starting to breathe. He doesn't wait for the obstetrician to spank him. As a matter of fact, most obstetricians no longer do this. If a baby has trouble breathing, they give him artificial respiration, very gently, with their hands or with a breathing apparatus.

The nurse tidies the baby up, takes his footprints, and attaches a beaded bracelet to his arm, with his parents' name on it, so everyone will know whose baby he is. Meanwhile, the obstetrician makes sure the mother is all right. Ready at hand just in case they are needed are drugs to stop bleeding and penicillin for use against infection.

Mrs. Rogers stays in the hospital for a week of well-earned rest and learns many things about baby feeding and care. Then she goes home with the new baby. Five weeks later the obstetrician gives her a final checkup. "I'm feeling fine," she says happily, "and so is the baby."

By this time the baby may be under the care of a children's doctor, or pediatrician. This doctor is an expert on the development from babyhood until the middle teens. He helps a mother work out a feeding schedule for the new baby and tells her when to start

giving orange juice and mashed vegetables. He keeps
a record of the growing child's height and weight
and of the immunizations he has had. The doctor
checks up on hearing and eyesight. He knows how
much sleep is necessary for good health and how important outdoor play is for developing a strong body.
At first the pediatrician advises the parents about
these things. When the children are old enough to
talk to, he coaches them in good health habits too.

"My doctor is like a first-rate counselor," one
twelve-year-old boy said. Pediatricians like children
and understand that while their bodies are growing
their feelings are changing too. A children's doctor is
pretty smart about the problems that come up at
home and school. He can sometimes offer good tips
on how to overcome shyness and make friends more
easily. He realizes the things that are on the mind of
a young person who is thinking of his life work and
the time when he will marry and have a home of his
own. It's good for anyone, young or old, to have an
understanding doctor with whom he can talk about
anything that's puzzling him.

Pediatricians treat the common children's diseases,
like mumps and measles, and the rarer diseases like
rheumatic fever. Attacks of rheumatic fever tend to
come back unless one is careful. Often they follow
a painful "strep" throat, so pediatricians are extra
careful to guard those who have had rheumatic fever
from throat infections. Some of these children receive

small doses of penicillin throughout the school year just as a precaution.

You can see that pediatricians spend a good deal of their time seeing that their young patients stay free of needless sickness. The healthiest time of life today is the ten years between ages five and fifteen. This was not always so. Now, though, so many childhood diseases are under control that the worst dangers left are automobile accidents, drowning, burns, falls, and loaded guns. Unfortunately, you can't vaccinate against accidents except by learning good safety habits.

Some doctors specialize in diseases of the organs inside the body. They become practitioners of internal medicine, or internists. An internist shouldn't be confused with an intern, who is a young doctor just through medical school and getting his first experience in a hospital. To become an internist, a doctor must have several years of advanced study and experience. Sometimes he specializes in just a single organ or system of the body, like the heart and blood vessels, the lungs, or the stomach and intestines.

If you know someone who suffers from hay fever, you may have heard him say, "I have an allergy to ragweed" (or something else). He sneezes and has watery eyes when the pollen is in the air, though it doesn't trouble most people at all. Perhaps he needs to see an allergist. This is a doctor who treats the sneezes or hives or wheezes that some people get when they inhale or eat whatever it is they are so sensitive to.

There are still more. A skin specialist is a dermatologist. A nerve specialist is a neurologist. Urologists treat diseases of the kidneys, bladder, and genito-urinary tract. The ear, nose, and throat doctor has the longest name of all. He's an otolaryngologist. When people hear a medical word like this, they often say, "It's Greek to me!" They're right. It *is* Greek. Many of the unfamiliar words doctors use come from this language—more even than from Latin. The most famous doctors of ancient times were Greeks, and even today, when a doctor discovers a new disease, he is likely to give it a Greek name.

Doctors sometimes speak of themselves as either physicians or surgeons. This is a little confusing, because in one sense "physician" can mean any doctor. In another sense it means a doctor who is not a surgeon.

A surgeon is a doctor who operates and removes diseased tissue so that it won't make trouble. He also makes repairs that give the body a chance to do its work the way it is supposed to. He mends broken bones and injured nerves and vessels. He makes new connections inside the body when old ones break down. He corrects defects that people may be born with. Once upon a time, children born with cleft palates could never learn to talk well, but now surgeons can repair this hole in the roof of the mouth very early in life.

There are all kinds of surgeons, just as there are all kinds of other doctors. Many family doctors do only simple surgery, like sewing up cuts. If a patient needs an important operation, they send him to a general surgeon. Besides these surgeons, who perform many kinds of operations, there are others who specialize.

Orthopedic surgeons correct defects of the joints and spine, sometimes by operation but more often with braces, supports, and corrective exercises. Plastic surgeons remove scars, build new noses and chins after bad injuries, and do all sorts of reconstruction jobs. There are eye surgeons, brain surgeons, and chest surgeons who operate on the lungs and heart. There are surgeons who open a new window into the inner ear to improve hearing. Imagine how hard some of these delicate operations are to do! Only a few surgeons learn the more difficult ones, and they must practice constantly to keep their skill.

Today surgeons can operate safely on newborn babies and on very old people. Sometimes a baby has a healthy appetite but can't hold anything on his stomach. He begins to waste away. Examination shows that the passage at the end of the stomach is closed tight by an overgrown muscle. An operation is necessary. The baby receives liquid and blood through a vein in the ankle until his strength is built up. Then the surgeon can operate and cut the tight muscle band. After this the baby is a perfectly normal child.

Old people can be built up for operations too. Dr. Paul H. Fluck, in the magazine, *Today's Health*, tells of an old man who had to have an operation for cancer. He was a crusty codger and felt sure his family was sending him to the hospital to die. So before he left, he made out a will, leaving all his money to his dog. He stayed in the hospital a long time and came out cured. He had also lost his fat paunch. The dog no longer recognized his master. He leaped at the old man and knocked him down. Back to the hospital went the patient with a broken hip. Again the surgeons fixed him up. The old man lived longer than his dog, and he changed his will, leaving his money once more to his family. At last he knew they had his interests at heart.

5

doctor teamwork

In the movies and on television you often see a physician or a surgeon fighting grimly to save a patient's life. The brilliant doctor seems to win out single-handedly against great odds. Every day doctors in real life gain victories as remarkable as these. But you seldom meet a doctor who claims all the credit for himself. Instead he says, "It was good teamwork that did the job." He was captain of the team, perhaps, but other doctors backed him up. So did nurses, technicians, and other people.

Most likely the patient never saw all the members of the team. Nevertheless, they were in there, fighting hard on his side.

One doctor the public seldom sees is the pathologist. He directs the hospital laboratories and the trained technicians, who do special tests of many kinds. Some are simple examinations of blood and urine, such as doctors often do in their own offices. Others are complicated tests that call for expensive hospital equipment.

Suppose a patient is too sick to swallow and has to receive fluids through a vein in the arm. His doctor wants to find out whether sodium and potassium, minerals necessary for life, are present in the right amounts or should be added to the fluid. He sends a blood sample to the laboratories, where an instrument called the flame photometer comes up with the right answer. This is how it works. First, a special solution is made from the blood. Then some of it is sprayed through an atomizer into the flame. Prisms catch the light of the flame and turn it into a rainbow-like band of colors. Photoelectric cells pick out the color of the burning sodium or potassium. A dial shows how much of the mineral is in the blood.

The pathologist supplies all sorts of useful information. In his laboratories you see racks of glass tubes with samples of blood used in what are called "sedimentation rate" tests. The red cells are settling to the bottom. Technicians are timing the rate at which these red cells fall. In some diseases the rate speeds up. Then, as the patient improves, it slows down again. Facts like these help a doctor keep tabs on how his patient is doing.

Chemical examinations of blood and urine show how well the kidneys are ridding the system of waste materials. Other tests may point a finger of suspicion at the liver, gall bladder, or certain glands—or give these organs a clean bill of health. Either way, the doctor wants to know. Finding out what the patient *doesn't* have wrong with him, is often a step toward learning what he *does* have.

The pathologist and his crew of workers never complain about unpleasant sights and smells, though they are careful to protect themselves from infection. It's part of the routine in the bacteriology laboratory to grow a colony of deadly germs from a sick patient's blood or sputum and then try out various antibiotics against the germs to see which one works best.

Pathologists do a great deal of "tissue work." After an operation, for example, they make a microscopic study of samples of the tissue the surgeon has removed. These findings go into the patient's record along with the opinion the surgeon wrote there *before* the operation. This is one of the ways doctors have of double-checking on the accuracy of their work.

It takes many steps to prepare tissue for mounting on a slide. Once in a while there is no time to wait. Suppose a surgeon is removing a tumor. He needs to know quickly whether it is cancerous or not. One of his assistants hurries to the pathologist with a sample of the tissue. Into a quick-freezing apparatus it goes, and out it comes in a moment, hard as a board. A machine slices off a paper-thin section, which the pathologist studies under the microscope for cancer cells. In a matter of minutes he sends the surgeon his report. If there is no cancer, the surgeon removes just the tumor. If it is cancer, he takes no chances but cuts away surrounding tissue to which the disease may have spread.

Another doctor on the team is the radiologist, or X-ray doctor. He too works mostly behind the scenes. When you have an X-ray taken, the person you meet may be an X-ray technician. The radiologist's main job is to decide what the X-ray pictures mean. He is likely to be in his office, dictating a report or standing in front of a lighted viewing box, discussing an X-ray plate with another doctor.

What is an X-ray plate? Is it a photograph of somebody's insides? Not exactly, because it takes light waves to make photographs. X-ray waves are much shorter and can pass through flesh and blood where light can't go. So X-ray pictures are called radiographs, not photographs.

Even X-rays can't pass through a bone or a hard, walled-off spot on the lungs. In a radiograph, such things show up in white on a black background. It is easy to see how valuable X-rays are in studying broken bones and lung diseases. The heart also is thick and dense enough so that the radiologist can see its shape and position.

For a long time it was hard to take a clear picture of other organs. X-rays passed through them, leaving only faint shadows on the plate. But today a radiologist knows how to look at almost any part of the inside of the body. If he needs to watch the digestive system at work, he gives the patient a "barium milk-shake" to drink. This looks like milk but doesn't taste like it, though the taste isn't really bad. The barium mixture is dense, and X-rays can't pass through it. As this odd "milkshake" passes down the esophagus into the stomach and on to the intestines, the radiologist or his technician takes pictures from time to time. Wherever the barium is, the digestive tract shows up white in clear outline. To the radiologist's trained eye, a little fleck of white may mean an ulcer. If an obstruction is present, he can see the barium detouring around it.

By using a fluoroscope, the radiologist can watch things while they happen. He looks at the lights and shadows that form as the X-rays strike the fluoroscopic screen. He sees the barium going down, swallow by swallow. A little later he watches the churning of the stomach and the rhythmic movement of the intestines. He can tell whether digestion is fast or slow. If anything on the screen looks suspicious, he touches a button and takes a picture for later study. Radiologists have even taken movies of digestion at work.

If a radiologist wants X-ray pictures of the spinal canal, he injects a special kind of oil, which makes the canal show up in white on the plate. An iodine mixture does the same for the blood vessels and the chambers of the heart. To take pictures of the kidneys and bladder, the radiologist shoots a little dye into an arm vein and waits for it to be excreted.

Looking at the gall bladder takes longer. The patient receives some tablets to swallow in the afternoon and comes back next morning without having eaten. The tablets contain a dye that passes through the walls of the intestines into the blood and on to the liver. The gall bladder, if it is working properly, picks up the dye from the liver. Then it shows up plainly by X-ray.

Information of this sort helps a doctor understand his patient the way a watchmaker knows the works of a watch. However, this is not the only way radiologists help other doctors. Sometimes they give special X-ray treatments. For this, they use machines of powerful voltage and direct a beam of rays at unhealthy tissue. Various skin conditions and other ailments are treated by X-ray, and also tumors and cancers deep inside the body.

People like to talk about their operations. An operation is a very good example of doctor teamwork. The surgeon, before he operates, first asks the family doctor all about the patient and studies the X-ray and laboratory reports. And he makes a careful examination of his own, for he wants to be sure the patient is in good condition for the operation.

Sometimes people are run down and need a few blood transfusions and some vitamins and proteins

3394

before an operation. The surgeon may ask the hospital's house staff to attend to these preparations. "House staff" means the interns and resident doctors who live at the hospital. They are young doctors who have finished medical school and are receiving advanced training under the direction of older doctors. Members of the house staff are on duty day and night in larger hospital and help patients in countless ways.

The anesthetist is a highly skilled member of the surgical team. Sometimes a nurse gives the anesthetic, sometimes a doctor. Often a doctor who has specialized in anesthesiology is in charge of this work at a hospital. He has an anesthetic for every purpose and chooses one as carefully as another doctor writes a prescription for medicine. Perhaps he decides to use a sleep-producing gas. For this he has a machine with tanks of ether and other gases, which he can combine with oxygen in any mixture. Instead of gas, he may select a drug that quickly brings on pleasant drowsiness and sleep. With other drugs, he can block off the pain nerves in a part of the body. If he injects a little anesthetic into the sheath of the spinal cord, the patient feels no pain from his lower abdomen to his toes.

Anesthesiologists have still other tools at their command. Sometimes they use a drug and a gas in combination. They have tamed the Indian arrow poison, curare. They don't use a dangerous dose of it, but

only enough to relax the muscles of the abdomen.
After a curare injection a patient needs only a small
amount of ether to pass into relaxed slumber. And
the more relaxed he is, the better the surgeon can do
his work.

Surgeons are about the cleanest, neatest people in
the world. Look at a surgeon's hands and notice how
soft the skin is and how the nails are pared down to
keep dirt from getting under them. When a surgeon
washes up for an operation, he really scrubs his hands
—and his arms too, up to the elbows. After using a
stiff brush and strong green soap or a germ-killing
solution, he holds his hands up so that the water will
run off the elbows, and dries them on a sterilized
towel. Then he must keep his hands above his waist
until the operation is over. A nurse helps him into a
gown and ties it behind him. His latex gloves are
rolled back part way so he can put them on without
touching the outside with his fingers.

All this care is not just for the sake of being fussy.
It is part of a life-saving plan doctors have worked
out to protect patients from infection during an operation. Germs that seldom do any harm on the skin or
in the nose and throat can be dangerous inside a
wound. So a surgeon goes to great pains to operate
in germ-free surroundings. The instruments, dressings, and sponges he uses and the linen that drapes the
table and the patient have been sterilized.

The team you see in photographs of operating

rooms usually has six members. The surgeon is at the side of the operating table, facing a doctor who is his first assistant and standing beside his second assistant. The anesthetist is at the head of the table and the instrument nurse toward the foot. In the background, away from the table, is the circulating nurse. Doctors jokingly call her the "dirty nurse," because she is allowed to handle unsterilized objects. No one else on the team may do this. When the circulating nurse brings a pack of supplies to the instrument nurse, she loosens the wrapping but never touches the sterilized things inside. The instrument nurse, for her part, mustn't touch the wrapping. She is the "clean nurse" and must stay that way.

Nothing is too much trouble if it safeguards the patient. The surgeon turns his head away from the table if he coughs, even though he has a mask over his mouth and nose. He is sure to perspire during a long operation, but he can't wipe away the sweat. Again he turns, and the circulating nurse mops his brow.

The patient is at the center of this drama, free from care. Before coming to the operating room, he received calming medicines. During the operation, and afterwards, the doctors take over for the patient. They watch his breathing, pulse, and heart. You might almost say the anesthetist breathes *for* the patient, for he knows just how much oxygen is flowing into the lungs and can change the amount at will. In fact, he *can* breathe for the patient, if necessary, by pumping the breathing bag that fills and empties during the operation.

The surgeon does his work very gently. He prides himself on losing as little of the patient's blood as possible, cutting no more than is necessary, and leaving the body tissues in good condition for healing. If he is taking out an appendix, he enters through the lower right abdominal wall, taking care not to cut across the muscles that lie beneath. Instead, he separates the muscles along the line of the fibers. Below he can see the membrane that covers the internal organs. He opens it and brings the inflamed appendix out into the wound. The big light overhead casts no shadow to hide his view.

The surgeon really works with several pairs of hands, for he is part of a team. His assistants hold back the muscles with instruments called retractors or help him clamp off arteries to stop the loss of blood. The instrument nurse seems to read the surgeon's mind and place the right instrument in his hands before he asks for it. Soon he has the appendix tied off at the base and ready to be cut. One move and out it comes. It will never make trouble for its owner again.

The instrument nurse has the surgeon's favorite needles and thread ready. He is an expert at sewing. Layer by layer, he brings the tissues together as they were before the operation. He may use fine silk thread or he may prefer catgut, which is really sheep gut. Surgeons know all kinds of stitches and can do work finer than any embroidery. Sometimes it is slippery work. Sewing up a blood vessel is like working on a piece of cooked macaroni, surgeons say.

After the operation is over, doctor-and-nurse teamwork continues to guard the patient. He may be wheeled to a nearby recovery room until he comes out of the anesthetic and has rested a while. Close at hand are oxygen, blood for transfusions, stimulants, mineral-containing fluids, and a suction device to clear out the breathing passage if necessary. Nothing has been overlooked.

The patient is in safe hands. He often gets up the next day, taking a few steps with the help of the nurse. And in a week he is home, talking to his friends about the operation.

"The surgeon was wonderful," he says, "and so were all the rest. They make a fine team."

6

community hospital:
a doctors' workshop

When a patient needs nursing care and special tests and treatments, his doctor usually sends him to a hospital. Everything is so handy there.

"The hospital is a doctors' workshop," doctors often say.

There are about seven thousand hospitals in the United States. Some are for veterans and the armed forces. Some are for patients with tuberculosis, mental illness, or other diseases that may last a long time. The rest—more than five thousand hospitals—are for people who generally stay only a few days.

If you visited one American hospital a day, it would take you twenty years to see them all. Here are the highlights of a tour through one hospital. It's not a big hospital and it's not a small hospital. It's in between.

This hospital is Greenwich Hospital and serves the

forty thousand people of Greenwich, Connecticut. Greenwich is a residential community thirty-two miles from New York City at the gateway to New England. The hospital, six stories high, is the tallest building in town. It stands on a wooded slope beyond the shopping center. Big windows are the first thing you see. The building is of white brick, but in the part where patients stay there is more glass than brick. You realize why after you get off the elevator at the top floor where the tour begins. The patients are lying in bed in the sunlit rooms, looking out through windows as wide as the rooms. They have a view of woods and water and white sailboats on Long Island Sound.

This top floor is for mothers and babies. In the nurseries, each baby has a glassed-off cubicle and its own thermometer, oil, and clothing. This is to make sure that no sickness spreads from one baby to another. No adult except baby nurses can go inside— not even doctors. When a doctor wants to examine a baby, the nurse brings it to him in a special room.

The most interesting nursery is the one for premature babies, or "preemies"—the ones who were born too soon. Some of them weigh only two or three pounds and are fed at first with an eye dropper. They need extra warmth and oxygen, so for a while they live inside an "isolette." It is a snug little glass house, with armholes for the nurse to reach through and care for the baby without making a draft.

"Preemies" stay in the hospital longer than other babies, but once they hit their stride they grow as fast as anybody. They just need building up with special feedings, blood transfusions, and lots of TLC.

Everybody in a hospital knows that TLC means "tender, loving care" and is a "must" for babies. In fact, it doesn't hurt anybody!

Greenwich Hospital has more than two hundred beds for patients. The largest rooms have four beds, and the others two beds or one bed. Hospital rooms used to have white walls, and some still do, but these rooms are decorated in cheerful colors, each room different. You wouldn't think you were in a hospital except for the nurses and doctors in white, coming and going.

Every room has running water and a toilet. Patients who are able to get out of bed like these conveniences. And so do the nurses, for nowadays they must save steps whenever they can. There are many new kinds of treatments, and the nurses help the doctors give them. To save time for these important duties, nurses have helpers themselves, such as aides and orderlies. At Greenwich Hospital and many other hospitals you also see women in bright-colored smocks taking patients to their rooms, delivering messages and flowers, and making things cheerful and pleasant all around. They are hospital volunteers who give several hours a week without pay to the work of their community hospital.

Patients who are getting well like to walk to the solarium, or sun room, and watch TV. During the World Series, everybody wants to know the score, even though he's still in bed. So at the end of each inning the score is broadcast over the public-address system. About all it says the rest of the year is "Calling Dr. Murphy" or the like.

The children's department has beds of three sizes —cribs, junior-size beds, and adult beds for teen-agers. There is also a playroom with toys, books, a record player, and a miniature movie screen. Children who have their tonsils out leave the hospital so soon they hardly have time to use it. But other things, like broken legs, take longer to mend.

A young patient who is to be in for several weeks thinks, "Well, no school for a while." He's wrong. Pretty soon a teacher comes to his bedside. She is there to see that pupils keep up with their lessons. Life goes on in a hospital much like anywhere else —only it's busier.

The doors are open all night and there are always lights at some of the windows. But the busiest time of all is around nine or ten in the morning when the doctors make their rounds. The doctor looks at the nurses' charts, where each patient's temperature, pulse, and general condition are written down. Then, one by one, he examines his patients and leaves new orders for tests and treatments.

Greenwich Hospital has the shape of a letter "T." Patients' rooms are along the top of the "T" where they get the southern sun. In the stem are workshops that serve the doctors' needs. One is the central sterile supply suite, with big metal doors in the wall like the entrance to a bank vault. Live steam under heavy pressure is at work behind these doors, sterilizing supplies that must be germ-free. Another sterilizer boils instruments. This busy workshop prepares supplies for the entire hospital, including the operating rooms on the floor below.

The best time to see these rooms is on an afternoon when operations are over for the day. The walls are finished in light green tile, because this is a restful color for surgeons' eyes. Everything is scrubbed and immaculate. The glass-doored cabinets are set back smooth with the wall so they won't catch dust.

Down another floor, you come to the laboratories and X-ray equipment. On most days the hospital does about two hundred laboratory tests. This section also has an electrocardiograph for studying the heart and a basal-metabolism apparatus. This last device measures the oxygen a person breathes and the heat his body gives off. Such information lets the doctor know how fast the body chemistry is working.

The X-ray department has several machines, one a deep therapy unit that operates at 220,000 volts. Big slabs of lead are in the walls around this machine for safety's sake. People who work around X-rays have to be especially careful not to absorb too much radiation. Sometimes you see them wearing badges that contain photographic film. When the film is developed, it shows whether too many X-rays are wandering around loose. If so, the equipment is checked at once to plug up the leak.

We come back to the main floor. There are no patients' beds here, but plenty is going on. Visitors are coming in through the front door. Two or three new patients are in the admitting office, arranging for their rooms. A mother with her new baby is going home. While she thanks the nurse for the good care she has received, father goes into the business office to pay the hospital bill. Down the corridor is the medical-records office, where the information that doctors have learned about their patients is kept for future use. In a little booth you see a doctor dictating his report into a recording machine. Also on this floor are a gift shop, soda fountain, cafeteria, several busy offices, and the rooms where doctors and other hospital people hold meetings.

One room is the administrator's office. It is his job to manage the hospital and see that everything runs properly. He understands how doctors work and what equipment they need to treat sick people. He knows many other things too, for the hospital has some four hundred employees in fifty different occupations. Downstairs below the main floor is a pharmacy which carries sixteen hundred kinds of drugs in stock. Two thousand additional items, from sheets to sugar, are kept in a storage room.

Just beyond a row of walk-in refrigerators is the

biggest kitchen in Greenwich, all agleam with stainless steel. At serving time, the patients' trays move along on a gliding belt between rows of food. Waitresses load the trays as they go by. Some of the trays carry little flags. A white flag means the doctor has ordered a liquid diet, a yellow flag is for a diabetic diet, and so on. A dietitian checks each tray, a boy whisks it into an insulated truck, and five minutes later the patient is sitting up in bed, eating a nice, hot dinner.

The hospital has a housekeeping staff to tidy up the rooms and polish miles of corridors. It has carpenters and painters to make repairs, and engineers who look after lighting, heat, power, ventilation, and refrigeration. A laundry washes and irons enough linen to amount to fifteen pounds a day for every patient. The diapers alone, if you hung them out, would fill a clothesline half a mile long. Actually they are tossed around in a tumbler to dry.

All these things add up to quite a workshop for the doctors. But the hospital is also a school for doctors and nurses. Student nurses work and study here for three years to become registered nurses. Interns and resident doctors study under the older doctors and learn by helping them. The older doctors study too, for no doctor ever gets too old and wise to stop learning. Every day lectures and classes are going on. Quite often specialists from other cities tell about new medical advances.

Nearly fifty doctors are on the regular staff of Greenwich Hospital, and many others have the privilege of treating their patients in the hospital. The doctors hold staff meetings to discuss difficult and complicated cases. This is a part of their never-ending education.

Some hospitals are city and county hospitals. Others are run by church groups or religious orders. Sometimes doctors have their own private hospitals. Greenwich Hospital is a community hospital. It is governed by a board of Greenwich citizens and is open to anyone in town who needs hospital care. Most of the patients pay for their care, but those who are too poor to do so are never turned away.

When patients get free hospital care, or pay only a small amount, it is the custom for doctors to treat them without charge. Doctors everywhere do a lot more free work than their neighbors know about. Patients who are poor may need a doctor, even though they are not sick enough to be in the hospital. In this case they visit a hospital clinic. Greenwich Hospital, for example, has twenty clinics for various kinds of illnesses. The clinic doctors are often able to clear up diseases before they become serious. Every doctor on the hospital staff gives some of his time to this work without pay.

Anybody, rich or poor, who has an accident may need a doctor in a hurry. You have probably noticed signs near hospitals pointing to the "emergency entrance" or "ambulance entrance." At Greenwich Hospital this entrance is at the foot of the slope on the side toward town. Here, below the rest of the building, is a little "hospital within a hospital." It has emergency operating rooms, recovery rooms, and plenty of splints, bandages, and other supplies.

You'd be surprised how many people get hurt and hurry to this emergency service for a doctor's help. Sometimes it's a bee sting, a dog bite, or a spill on a slippery rug. Sometimes it's food poisoning or sudden illness. One man fell out of a tree that he was pruning. He went way out on a limb, forgot where he was, and sawed off the limb he was sitting on. Fortunately he was not badly hurt, because accidents are sometimes very serious. Now and then a young child is carried in, scalded from head to foot after pulling a kettle of hot soup off the stove. Or there is an automobile collision, and six people arrive by ambulance, some of them badly injured.

On an ordinary day, twenty-four emergency patients reach Greenwich Hospital. This amounts to one an hour, day and night, only no one knows when they are coming. So the emergency service is always open. Doctors are always ready to swing into action and alert the rest of the hospital if necessary.

7

new-style country doctors

Like everyone else, young doctors who are finishing
their studies enjoy a "bull session" now and then.
They like to get together and talk about their plans.
Some want to practice medicine in the city. Others
prefer the country. Perhaps they enjoy living near
lakes and woods. Or they realize that farmers, fishermen, lumbermen, and miners need doctors just as
much as city people do.

It isn't always easy for a doctor to decide where
to go. He may have spent several years learning to
be an orthopedic surgeon. He would like to settle in
the country but wonders whether there are enough
people needing his special skills to keep him busy.
Wouldn't it be more sensible, he asks himself, to
open an office in the city, where there are opportunities for all kinds of doctors?

If you were to listen in while two young doctors
discussed their plans, you might hear a conversation
something like this:

"I'd sure like to practice in the country."

"Leave that to the general practitioners. You're a specialist. People who live in the country can't afford a lot of specialists. They're lucky to have even one doctor."

"Country people get sick the same as city people. Why shouldn't they have any kind of medical service they need?"

"It's not practical. Listen, Mac, you are used to the best equipment and the finest laboratories. You would have nothing to work with in the country. At the very least, you'd need an up-to-date hospital. It would cost a million dollars."

"There must be a simpler way to begin. I'd still like to practice in the country."

No doubt there have been hundreds of conversations like this—and many of them have gone no farther. For how could one doctor, all by himself, get the expensive equipment needed to practice a specialty? How could he find enough patients to make a living in a little country town?

Still, there *is* an answer to these perplexing questions. Hospitals that are really little medical centers are springing up in many places. They are located in a town or in a small city, but they also serve the country round about. Doctors of many kinds share in the use of the fine laboratories and other advantages that are to be found in these centers. They can be city doctors and country doctors at the same time.

The story of Thayer Hospital, in Waterville, Maine, tells how one such center came to be.

Waterville is a thriving little city on the Kennebec River and the stepping-off place for a lot of country. Up the river valley is Moosehead Lake and the big game country of the north Maine woods. It is 117 miles from Waterville to the Canadian border. Cars loaded with canoes and hunting or fishing gear travel the road in the summer and fall, but snow lies deep on the hillsides in winter. This is when the lumber camps come to life, and tractors pull spruce logs over the snow to the frozen streams. When the ice breaks up in the spring, the logs float down to paper mills along the Kennebec. There is a big paper mill in Waterville and several cotton and woolen mills. In the country close by are many poultry and dairy farms.

It happened that half a dozen of the Waterville doctors used to lunch together frequently. Naturally they fell into the habit of comparing ideas and "talking shop." Whenever a doctor went to a medical meeting and heard about new discoveries, he told the other doctors about it when he came back. They were all anxious to keep up with the times.

One day a doctor said, "We make a good team. Too bad we don't have a hospital where we could work together more closely and carry out our ideas. But I guess it would cost a million dollars."

"Maybe we don't need a million dollars," said another doctor.

Shortly before this, an elderly physician named Dr. Thayer had died, and his home was for sale. It was an old-fashioned gabled house that had lots of room. The six doctors borrowed money to buy it. They added on an extension and made the building over into a little hospital of thirty-five beds. A young nurse, Miss Pearl Fisher, became the superintendent.

It was a simple place, but teamwork helped make up for the lacks. My first visit to Thayer Hospital was in the summer of 1947. By this time, the half-dozen doctors had grown in number to sixteen. Some were general practitioners, some were specialists. Patients were now coming to the hospital not only from Waterville but from many parts of central and northern Maine. So there was plenty for all the doctors to do.

Each doctor who joined the Thayer team agreed to follow the hospital rules. He promised to share his knowledge and experience at all times. If another doctor called him in on a case, the most he could charge for the consultation was five dollars—no matter how much of a specialist he was. If the patient couldn't afford five dollars, he gave his services for nothing. Something else he did free was to hurry to a special meeting every couple of weeks. These meetings were called whenever a hospital patient was so sick that his life was in danger. The sixteen doctors discussed what ought to be done. Nobody was allowed to die if any doctor knew how he could be saved.

Maine has cool summers most of the time, but the day of my visit was a scorcher. The offices and mills in town closed early so that people could go home and cool off. But a hospital can't close. Two patients came in during the hot afternoon for emergency appendix operations. There was a shortage of nurses, so Miss Fisher, the superintendent, put on her mask and cap and joined the surgeon's team. Later that evening two babies were born. It was nearly midnight when Miss Fisher quit for the day.

The doctors held their regular weekly meeting that evening and let me listen in. Despite the weather there was a full attendance—except for the doctor who was upstairs delivering the babies.

"People get sick in the summer too," said one of the doctors.

During the evening, the chairman of the meeting called on ten doctors and asked each of them to tell about a patient who was then in the hospital. After the report there was a discussion of the case. If one doctor didn't agree with another, he said so, but no one had his feelings hurt. They were all friends and they were there to learn.

Waterville is near the Belgrade Lakes where there

are more than a hundred vacation resorts and children's camps. Anyone who slips on a diving board, or cuts his foot on a broken bottle, or breaks out with poison ivy is likely to be brought to Thayer Hospital for emergency treatment. Summer is a busy time when almost anything can happen. One of the doctors had just taken a hellgrammite from a young man's eyelid. A hellgrammite is a many-legged wriggler that fishermen use for bait. The patient, in casting out his line, had snagged his own eyelid. So the doctor removed hook and hellgrammite, and patient took his bait and went back fishing.

It was haying time, and a farmer was in the hospital with an injured hand. He had hurt it in a baling machine. It required painstaking surgery to sew up the tendons and reset the tiny broken bones of the hand. But the farmer's living depended on having good hands, and the doctors did not fail him.

Other doctors had recently saved a baby's life. To do this, they had to make an almost complete switch in the baby's blood. The infant was born "RH-positive"—it had antibodies from the mother's blood that were destroying its own red cells. It was necessary to remove the baby's blood, little by little, and put in blood of a different kind. Thus gradually, by many transfusions through a tiny vein in the scalp, the baby received a new supply of blood.

The blood donor was a mechanic who was driving

to a job with his car radio on. He heard an appeal for blood of a special type. Being a war veteran, he knew his type and hurried to the hospital.

"Why shouldn't I help?" he exclaimed. "My wife was saved at Thayer Hospital last year."

It was seven years before my next visit to this hospital in 1954. Thayer Hospital had moved to a brand-new modern building on a beautiful site near Colby College. Here it has twice as many beds as in the old location. Everything is bright and shiny. The X-ray department and laboratories are big enough for a much larger hospital. And no wonder. Thayer Hospital does complicated laboratory tests for eight other hospitals in Maine.

Up in the north woods the lonely villages are fifty miles and more from a hospital. In country like this, a single doctor serves a big territory. He can't hope to own all the equipment a hospital has. But he can always send a patient to the diagnostic clinic at Thayer Hospital. Specialists here do a complete examination and send their findings to the patient's doctor, along with suggestions for treatment.

So patients are constantly arriving at Waterville for diagnosis. They come from many parts of the state of Maine—by car, train, and bus. A lumberman from up near Canada had just landed on the stream near the hospital on the pontoons of his private plane.

Country doctors and town doctors also send patients to Thayer Hospital for difficult operations. During my visit a car drove up and the chauffeur led an elderly man into the hospital. The older man was nearly blind and had come for an operation on his eyes. Very likely it was for the removal of cataracts. These are growths which sometimes interfere with the sight of older people. A skillful eye surgeon can cut them away and restore sight. His cataract knife is probably the sharpest knife in the world. Its tiny blade must be tested before every operation. One way to do this is to stretch a very thin piece of kidskin over the top of a jelly glass and hold it tight with a rubber band. The skin looks like flimsy cleaning tissue. The surgeon plunges his knife into it. If it cuts clean, the knife is sharp. If the tear is jagged, it's not sharp enough yet.

Thirty doctors now work at Thayer Hospital, including almost every kind of specialist. Besides helping city folk, they are also new-style country doctors. They help bring the latest advances of medical science to the farmers, lumberjacks, mill workers, and other residents of a big chunk of Maine.

The new hospital really cost a million dollars—in fact, a little more. Many people in the Waterville region made gifts of money so it could be built. They knew the value of the hospital by now.

The doctors' meetings at Thayer Hospital are so interesting that visiting doctors from other places often drive fifty or seventy-five miles to attend.

"It helps you keep up with what's going on in medicine," they say.

Thayer Hospital has become a good health center. Doctors from all over the state, and sometimes from other states, hold meetings there. Boston University sends student nurses to Thayer during part of their course so they will learn about rural nursing.

The hospital runs many clinics in cooperation with the State Department of Health. One is for crippled children. Another is an eye clinic, where children with crossed eyes are helped while they are still very young. There is a clinic for children who have trouble speaking clearly. If you passed by, you might see them blowing bubble gum or tooting horns. This is a lesson in better control of the lips, tongue, and breath. Each week eighty-five Maine youngsters come to a hard-of-hearing clinic. A therapist teaches them how to read lips and how to say words, so that they can go to school.

Thayer Hospital doctors give their services at these clinics without pay. Sometimes clinics are held in other parts of the state, and they travel there to be of help too.

The dream of bringing the latest and best in medical care to the country is coming true. Doctors, nurses, and hospital people visit Thayer Hospital to learn the secret of its success. They are from all over the country, even from foreign lands. One recent visitor was from Helsinki, Finland. Another was from Bagdad in Iraq. A visiting doctor from Nepal practices in a village near the foot of Mount Everest.

Even in the United States there are many country districts where doctors are too far away from good hospitals and other advantages. So the Alfred P. Sloan Foundation made a movie not long ago about the work of Thayer Hospital. The American Hospital Association lends the film to people in small towns and rural areas who want to see what the Maine doctors did. The film is called, *Why Wait for a Million?*

8

clinics, large and small

A stranger, driving through the Minnesota dairy country, stopped at a filling station.

"Is there a doctor in town?" he asked the attendant.

"Mister, are you kidding?" came the reply. "There are five hundred doctors in this town."

Such a conversation might take place any day in Rochester, Minnesota. The town has thirty thousand people and more doctors than any other place of its size in the world. It is the home of the famous Mayo Clinic. Some two hundred and fifty doctors are on the staff of this clinic. An equal number of young doctors are studying at the clinic and in the hospitals of this doctors' town.

For every person who lives in Rochester, a hundred or more have visited the clinic as patients. They come from every state in the Union and from many foreign lands.

The Rochester airport is an important stop on air routes connecting at Seattle with the Far East and in New York with Europe. The planes level off over cow pastures and red barns, then land on a former corn field. Among the passengers who step down may be an admiral with high blood pressure and a maharajah who needs a gall-bladder operation. They ride into town in the airport limousine with an allergic movie actress, a ball player with a bad arm, and a noted British surgeon. The surgeon has come to watch how a new operation is done.

The limousine makes stops at several big hotels. The hospitals—St. Mary's and Rochester Methodist—are even bigger than the hotels. And the Mayo Clinic is bigger than the hospitals. It is fifteen stories high, not counting a bell tower that rises four stories more. Tunnels connect it with the hospitals and hotels. The Mayo Clinic is the center of the town.

Most of the patients who visit the Mayo Clinic come because their home-town doctors sent them. If a man has a brain tumor, his doctor may tell him, "I'll arrange for you to go to the Mayo Clinic for an operation by a specialist."

Perhaps another doctor is stumped by a rare illness. "Why don't you run out to the Mayo Clinic and get the works?" he suggests. "If anybody can find the trouble, they can."

Sometimes a doctor has to tell a patient, "As yet, no cure is known for your condition."

"Isn't there anything I can do, doctor?" asks the patient.

"Well, you might try the Mayo Clinic. They are doing some research on this disease out there. Don't get your hopes up. But there's a bare chance—"

Conversations like these start thousands of patients on their way to the Mayo Clinic every year. Each new patient receives a thorough examination, no matter what appears to be the trouble. It may be something quite different from what he thinks. Or perhaps the trouble he already knows about has hidden complications. So the patient is checked by one doctor after another. He goes to laboratories for tests and X-rays. Strange-looking recording devices measure the electrical impulses from his muscles or brain. Specialists follow up every clue and talk to one another about their findings.

Some patients come to the clinic for diagnosis only. This takes two or three days, or sometimes longer. The doctors figure out where the trouble lies and what can be done about it. They send this information to the patient's home-town doctor. Then the patient goes home for treatment. Other patients stay for a course of treatments or an operation by clinic surgeons.

Rochester is full of cars with out-of-state license plates. Some are shiny new Cadillacs, but there are little Chevvies and battered old Buicks, too. You may see a mother coming out of the bus station, carrying a broken suitcase and leading a sick child.

The doctors know that not everyone who comes

to the Mayo Clinic is a millionaire. The Cadillac owner may pay a thousand dollars and the man with the jalopy only three hundred. The mother with the sick child doesn't get a bill at all. If three men are sitting outside a laboratory waiting for a blood test, one may be a Kansas farmer, one a retired railroad conductor, and one a United States Senator. Each man waits his turn and gets the same careful attention.

The Mayo Clinic grew from the practice of an old-fashioned horse-and-buggy doctor. This first Dr. Mayo was Dr. William Worrall Mayo, who came to Minnesota as a pioneer and settled in Rochester. His two sons, Will and Charlie, often went with him on his calls. They helped their father dress wounds, mix medicines, and set broken limbs. Later they went to medical school and became doctors themselves. Actually they had been learning to be doctors from the time they could walk. They learned doctoring the way farm boys learn farming.

In time, some of their father's patients moved out to the new frontier in the Dakotas, but they missed old Dr. Mayo. So when they got sick they came back on the new railroad to see him. The old doctor was so busy that his sons took over many of the new cases. People began talking about "going to the Mayos." To tell the doctors apart, they called them "Old Dr. Mayo," "Dr. Will," and "Dr. Charlie."

Dr. Will and Dr. Charlie were frontiersmen like many of their patients. The frontier the young doctors were exploring was that of surgery. After 1890, this frontier moved ahead rapidly. Doctors now knew about germs and were careful to keep surgical wounds clean. Operations became safer, and new operations were developed to help conditions that had been incurable in the past.

The Mayo brothers were eager to master this new knowledge. They made trips to Chicago, Philadelphia, and Boston to watch great surgeons at work and learn from them. Dr. Will paid particular attention to operations on the abdomen and Dr. Charlie to operations on the nose, throat, and head. After a while they became known as great surgeons themselves. More patients came to the Mayos for operations than they could take care of. So Dr. Will and Dr. Charlie invited other skillful surgeons to join their team. Gradually, in this way, the Mayo Clinic came into being. Others besides surgeons were needed on the team—pathologists, radiologists, internists, doctors of all kinds.

Dr. Will and Dr. Charlie were famous, but they never got puffed up with their own importance. They weren't impressed by wealth or fame. To them, one sick person was as important as another. People in Rochester still tell about the man who thought he was too important to wait in line when he arrived at the clinic. Much annoyed, he bustled up to Dr. Will in the lobby and asked, "Are you the head doctor here?" Replied Dr. Will, "No, my brother Charlie is the head doctor. I'm the belly doctor."

Dr. Will and Dr. Charlie both died in 1939, but the Mayo Clinic lives on as one of the world's great medical centers. Doctors of many kinds work there. Some spend most of their time diagnosing and treating patients. Some are teachers. Their pupils are "fellows"—young doctors who are doing postgraduate work in a medical specialty. Other Mayo doctors are investigating some disease or scientific problem. Two Mayo men—a physician and a biochemist—discovered the drug cortisone and its use in rheumatoid arthritis.

The Mayo Clinic was an early example of what is now called "group practice." Medical students sometimes ask each other, "Are you going in for solo practice or group practice?" A doctor who sets up his own office is in solo practice. If he joins with several other doctors who practice together, he is in group practice.

Of course, hardly any doctor is entirely "solo" these days. He consults with other doctors and sends his patients to them for special examinations. He works closely with other doctors at the hospital and discusses difficult cases at medical meetings. When he goes to a medical convention or takes a vacation, he asks another doctor to take care of his patients while he is away. Any major operation, as we have seen, calls for teamwork by a number of doctors.

Some doctors prefer to practice as part of a team all the time. They get together with several other doctors and organize a medical group. There are five hundred or more of these medical groups in the United States today. More of them are in Minnesota than in any other state. Perhaps this is because of the example of the Mayo Clinic. Group practice by doctors is fairly common in the Middle West, the South, and the West. It has grown more slowly in the New England and Middle Atlantic states.

There are various kinds of medical groups. Some draw patients from many places. Others are chiefly for the home-town people. Some groups do nothing but treat eye diseases, or cancer, or make difficult diagnoses. Many give general medical care.

Medical groups are often called "clinics." The word "clinic" has several meanings. When a teacher in medical school brings some patients before his class, so that the students can see what a certain disease looks like, or how to treat it, that is a clinic. Doctors also hold clinics for the purpose of treating patients who cannot afford to pay a private physician. Nowadays any place where several doctors work together is likely to be called a clinic. If you see a sign reading "Jones Clinic," it may mean that old Dr. Jones has such a big practice that he needs a couple of younger doctors to help him. Or it may mean that several doctors have formed a medical group.

A typical group has from six to twelve doctors

in it. Two or three are likely to be general practitioners or specialists in internal medicine. The others may be a general surgeon, an obstetrician, and a pediatrician. The group also needs a pathologist and a radiologist part of the time. So it may arrange for men in these specialties to divide their time between the clinic and their other work. As a group increases in size, it adds other specialists, as well as more physicians and surgeons.

The group very likely has a business manager, who need not be a doctor. In fact, doctors are usually glad to let someone else keep the accounts and collect the bills. Then of course there will be office nurses, technicians, receptionists, and other helpers, depending on the size of the group. A clinic with a dozen doctors begins to look like a little hospital, only there are no beds for staying overnight.

Group practice is one way of bringing together all the different and remarkable skills of doctors. When a patient "goes to see the doctor" at a group clinic, he actually sees several doctors. If he is worried about a wheeze, he may be examined by a general practitioner, a throat specialist, and an allergist, and have a chest X-ray—all on the same visit. Everything is under one roof. He doesn't have to go from one part of town to another, seeing different doctors. Being thoroughly examined is so easy that people sometimes find out about a disease in the early stages when it is easier to cure. Doctors who work in a group often say they like it because they can spend more time at home with their families. This is because members of a group take turns answering night calls and emergencies.

Of course, doctors who work together so closely have to be good friends, and know how to stay that way, or they get on one another's nerves. Many doctors say, "I want to practice solo so I can be my own boss." Patients sometimes say, "I want a doctor I can call my own doctor. In a group I'd feel like a case with a number." Medical groups recognize this need, and in some of them, every patient has a "personal physician." This is the doctor he sees first whenever he visits the clinic. He may see other doctors too, but after the various examinations are finished he comes back to his personal doctor to talk things over.

Thus he has several doctors but one of them is something special—a trusted friend who knows his aches and pains and to whom he can always turn.

9

doctors where you work

"No one here has lost an eye from accidents in ten years," said the doctor at the Sperry Gyroscope Company. He was not superstitious but he knocked on wood anyway. The streak of luck was too good to risk breaking!

It wasn't all luck, though. Inside the glass case on the wall were many pairs of smashed safety glasses. The lenses of some were cracked. Others were crunched up, like safety glass in an automobile windshield after a collision. Each pair of glasses had done its work well. It had shielded someone's eyes from steel splinters, molten metal, or a blow from a moving object. Sometimes both lenses were smashed. This meant that a man had probably been saved from total blindness.

Eighteen thousand men and women work in the huge Sperry Gyroscope plant at Great Neck, Long Island, not far from New York City. Many of them need eye protection on their jobs. On his way to the machine shops a man thinks, "It's a nuisance to put on goggles." Then he passes the case of smashed glasses and sees how some fellow-employees' sight was saved. "Better not take a chance," he says—and reaches for his glasses.

This is one of many ways that the doctors of this company guard the health of the employees. The medical department at Sperry Gyroscope is an example of what many companies are doing to keep people healthy on the job. It is like a small hospital, all spic-and-span, with treatment rooms, laboratories, X-ray and physical-therapy equipment, and beds for anyone who gets sick or hurt. This spot is part of the first home of the United Nations, which met here before moving to New York City.

Four doctors work full time for the Sperry Gyroscope medical department, and eight others part time. Helping them are twenty-five nurses, technicians, and receptionists. Every day several hundred employees come here to "see the doctor" for whatever ails them. Sometimes it's a cut hand or a wrenched ankle. More often it's a headache or a cold getting started. In summertime it may be a heat rash or poison ivy, in wintertime a bad cough or a spill on the ice on the way to work. Monday morning brings in people with bumps and bruises from week-end play or upset stomachs from something they ate.

Sometimes the doctor tells the employee to go home until he is well. More often, some medicine

and a little rest make the patient feel better. Then
he can go back on the job without losing time from
work. It's a company doctor's job to help people
while they are on the job, and he doesn't try to take
the place of a family doctor. If an employee doesn't
have a doctor to look after his family's health, the
company doctor urges him to get one.

If you ever apply for a job at Sperry Gyroscope,
you will receive a thorough medical examination before you go to work. The doctors are not looking
for an excuse to turn you down. They want to make
sure that no one is given work that might damage
his health or endanger others. For example, a man
with blind spots in his field of vision shouldn't be a
company chauffeur, though he would be all right
in some other jobs.

As a matter of fact, several totally blind persons
work at Sperry Gyroscope. Instead of their eyes,
they use their sense of touch to assemble delicate instruments. War veterans with legs missing have sit-
ting-down jobs. In the company cafeteria you see
women making salads and pushing food carts. They
are as spry as can be, though several are more than
seventy years of age. Two are past eighty!

Thus the medical department helps fit people to
jobs they can do safely. A worker who is out sick
for more than a week gets a new examination on his
return. The doctors at Sperry Gyroscope are always
hearing about people's troubles—not only health

problems, but job and home worries too. They offer sympathy and helpful advice along with their medicine. Anything that stops worry makes a person feel better on the job.

Company doctors try to stop trouble before it starts. They work with the safety engineers to prevent accidents. They make sure that machinery is properly lighted, investigate complaints, and study the plant for every possible danger. When an accident happens, they try to figure out how to keep it from happening again. Men who work with harsh chemicals are examined from time to time and are put on a new job at the first sign of injury to their skin.

An ambulance and two station wagons are waiting at different parts of the big plant—ready to rush anyone who needs help to the medical department.

Most big plants have medical departments. But how about people who work for a small company? They get sick and hurt too. Can they have a doctor on the job?

This is not so easy to arrange in a plant that can't afford a full-time doctor, but it can be done. A few years ago eight small companies got together and hired the full-time services of a doctor who was interested in industrial medicine. Today each company has its own little medical department with a nurse on duty all the time. Each day the doctor calls at four of the plants and stays a couple of hours. It takes him two days to make the rounds of all eight plants. But if there is an emergency anywhere, the nurse telephones the doctor, and he jumps into his car and is there in a hurry.

Many companies have a full-time nurse but only a part-time doctor. The medical department may be only a cubbyhole with space curtained off into a waiting room and a couple of examining rooms. Still, having a doctor and a nurse around makes all the difference in the world. People like to know there is a place close at hand where they can drop in for medical aid.

Some of the smallest factories of all are located in the heart of New York City within five minutes' walk of Pennsylvania Station. Here, within a few blocks, are some eight thousand "shops," as they are called, turning out dresses, coats, blouses—just about everything women wear from nightgowns to ski suits. Most of these little factories are in loft buildings or skyscrapers. Many have only twenty-five or thirty employees.

This is quite different from Sperry Gyroscope with eighteen thousand workers. But then Sperry Gyroscope makes instruments with parts that have to be exactly alike. Who ever heard of women all wanting the same kind of dress? They'd rather have many designs to choose from. So there are lots of small factories, all trying to do something different. If you add them together, though, there are a lot of people at work making ladies' garments—two hundred thousand in New York City alone.

What do these two hundred thousand garment workers do for a doctor on the job? You couldn't find room for a doctor among the noisy sewing machines and heaped-up dress goods in eight thousand separate workrooms.

But take a short walk from anywhere in the garment district, stop at 275 Seventh Avenue, and you will see a twenty-seven-story building with big letters in front reading "Union Health Center." This building belongs to the International Ladies Garment Workers Union. More than two thousand union members come here every day to see a doctor. The Union Health Center is really a medical department for all those thousands of dress shops and the people who work in them. The union and the shop owners have an agreement that for every dollar of wages, a few extra pennies go for the expenses of the Health Center. It occupies seven floors of the building and is growing all the time.

The Union Health Center is always a busy place, but it's the busiest of all after work, from five to seven o'clock, and on Saturdays when the shops are shut down. It has fifty-eight examining rooms. Outside are comfortable chairs for waiting, with flowers and plants to look at and gay-colored health posters to read. One hundred seventy-six doctors are on duty at the Center, and ten of them spend all their

time here. So no matter what a garment worker's
health problem may be, he is sure to find a doctor
who is an expert on the subject.

Some problems, like eyesight, are especially important in this industry. Garment workers often call
themselves "needle workers." The needle is an important tool of their trade, even when it is built into
a power sewing machine. A woman needs sharp eyes
to thread the needle at a distance of eight inches and
then guide the work through the racing machine at
twice that distance. A man who operates a cutting
machine needs clear vision too. One minute he is
slicing through a pile of cloth right under his nose.
An instant later the work is at arm's length. If he
needs glasses, ordinary reading glasses won't do. He
has to have special glasses so that he can see at different distances. Eye specialists at the Union Health
Center, who know what each job is like, prescribe
such glasses.

People who are on their feet all day pressing garments or cleaning off spots have problems too. If
their feet ache or their posture is bad, they can get
help in the orthopedic clinic at the Center.

The physical-therapy suite has twenty-three
rooms for special baths and other treatments. Needle
workers need nimble fingers; if the finger joints become stiff, it is a serious handicap. So one of the
treatments is a finger bath. The patient dips his fingers into a tank containing dissolved paraffin. When

he takes them out, his fingers are covered with a warm coating that feels like wax from a burning candle. It stays warm quite a while, relieves the pain, and makes it easier to exercise the fingers.

The Union Health Center tries to help people get well and stay well. There is a nutrition clinic to which doctors send patients who need to change their eating habits. Some don't drink enough water or milk or eat enough fresh vegetables and citrus fruits. Others try to do a hard day's work on a skimpy breakfast. The clinic has a kitchen where the nutritionist shows patients how to prepare healthful foods. Wax models of various food servings show what "a quarter of a pound of meat" or "a small potato" really looks like. And there are leaflets like one on "cool drinks for hot days" that shows which beverages contain minerals and vitamins and which do not.

Workers who come to the Union Health Center for the first time, as well as those who return for physical checkups, receive the usual blood and other examinations so that hidden disease may be caught and treated. But this isn't all. As an additional protection, everyone gets a miniature chest X-ray. Usually there is nothing the matter, but once in a while the doctor notices something about the lungs or heart that calls for further examination. In this way tuberculosis may be discovered in the early stages when it can be most successfully treated.

The battle against tuberculosis in the garment industry is steadily being won, but it has been a long fight. Older men and women remember the "sweatshop" days when this disease was an ever-present danger to every needle worker. Men, women, and children worked ten hours or more a day, including Sundays, in firetrap buildings and crowded slum dwellings. The dirty, unswept rooms were lighted by gas jets. Little fresh air and sunlight got in. The sweatshops were hot in summer and freezing in winter. Workers who became sick had no doctor to go to. They kept on working and coughing. Tuberculosis spread to others in the shop.

Now all this is changed. The garment workers are proud of their good working conditions and of their Union Health Center. They have far better health than their parents did. Dr. Leo Price, who has been director of the Center for many years, has seen much of this improvement with his own eyes and has heard about it from his father, who was also a doctor and who started the Center back in 1913. Tuberculosis was then "the great white plague." Needle workers suffered from it perhaps more than any other group. Today the younger Dr. Price can hope that before many years tuberculosis will be a thing of the past. "Routine X-rays periodically for every adult," he says, "would soon make tuberculosis as rare as smallpox."

10

live with what you have

"Get out of that wheel chair and walk!" said the doctor in a gruff voice.

The little girl with her legs in braces saw the smile on the doctor's face and knew he was only pretending to be cross. She grasped the arms of the chair, pulled herself upright, and proudly took five steps into her mother's arms.

"It's the first time I've seen her walk since she had polio!" exclaimed the delighted mother.

Scenes like this occur all the time in the waiting room of the Institute for Physical Medicine and Rehabilitation in New York. It is part of the New York University-Bellevue Medical Center, which covers many blocks of a neighborhood a mile south of the United Nations.

The Institute is more like a school than a hospital. All the "pupils" have handicaps that remained with them after they were sick or hurt. Some are as young as two. Others are as old as seventy. You never saw so many wheel chairs in your life. They come equipped with brakes for quick stopping, because a rider who knows how to work the hand rims can streak down the hall faster than a man can run. A wheel chair with balloon tires does pretty well even on a dirt road.

Still, a wheel chair has drawbacks. You can't get in and out of a bathtub in a wheel chair, or wriggle through a crowded bus to the exit door. Patients at the Institute, even those with paralyzed legs, want to be able to move around freely and take care of themselves.

The Institute has beds for sixty patients. Others come in for special treatments.

Three-year-old Brenda of Tazewell, Virginia, had cerebral palsy and couldn't sit up or stand up. When she tried to move, her arms and legs flew out in unexpected directions. At the Institute she learned to sit in a chair and feed herself. Then, with braces on her legs and body, she practiced walking. Her arm movements became surer as she played with building blocks. Instead of lying helpless in bed, she will go to school like everyone else.

Lieutenant Aldo Borzaga lost both legs from frostbite after being trapped in a blizzard in August. This happened in the mountains of Argentina. It was wintertime there, and the lieutenant was on army maneuvers. Though his feet were frozen, he saved the lives of seven men and was decorated by his government for bravery. Later he came to the Institute and learned to walk skillfully on artificial legs.

Paul Francolon was a famous French jockey. In 1946 he fell from a horse and broke his back. After that he was a paraplegic, a person who is paralyzed below the waist. Francolon spent six years in a wheel chair. Then he heard about the Institute and came to New York by plane. He learned to balance himself on crutches and swing his weight from his arms and shoulders. When Francolon returned to France, he could go up and down stairs with the aid of two canes. Also he had learned watchmaking and knew he could always make a living.

Miss Edith Kenny is a pretty secretary at the Institute. The patients admire her because she is a patient who has made good. To look at Miss Kenny, you can hardly believe that she spent twenty years in a wheel chair. Yet she did. As a young girl, Edith had a bad case of polio. People said she would never be able to work. Twenty years later the Institute proved they were wrong. Miss Kenny showed so much pluck and progress as a patient that the Institute asked her to stay on there and work.

Bob was a college student. One day he did a high dive into a swimming pool. It was shallower than he thought, and Bob hit his head and broke his neck. He was in bad trouble because his leg muscles would not work and neither would his arm muscles. "Bob's schooldays are over. He can't even write," thought friends. But at the Institute Bob learned to write without hands. He did this by holding a plastic rod in his teeth and tapping the keys of an electric typewriter. Bob became such a good typist that he was able to go back to college and keep up with his work.

Mr. Roberts, an elderly man, suffered a stroke which damaged part of his brain. This left him paralyzed on the right side. He might have spent the rest of his life in bed. Instead he came to the Institute and learned to write, eat, brush his teeth, and shake hands with his left hand. He gets about with a cane and runs his business as usual.

The man who directs the Institute is Dr. Howard A. Rusk. Other doctors and therapists of various kinds work with him. During World War II, Dr. Rusk was in charge of convalescent training for the Air Force. He saw thousands of flyers who had been wounded in action. With marvelous skill, surgeons had saved their lives. But often some disability remained that could not be cured on the operating table—a missing limb, a severed spinal cord, or lost eyesight.

Yet there was one thing that could not be disabled, Dr. Rusk learned, and that was ambition. Men who had the will to live the best lives they could were able to conquer severe handicaps.

The results were so encouraging that after the war Dr. Rusk and others who had worked with him started the present Institute for Physical Medicine and Rehabilitation. "Physical medicine" means exercise, baths, massage, heat and electrical treatments, and other methods doctors use so that disabled people can take better care of themselves. When they are able to go to school, or get a job, or keep house, they are said to be "rehabilitated."

Dr. Rusk believes that a person always has more left than he has lost. "Let's see what you can do with what you have left," he says.

"Live with what you have left" is a guiding motto at the Institute.

Each new patient is examined to see what he *does* have left. How strong are his muscles? How limber are his joints? How much can he move his arms and legs? Even more important, how does he *feel* about his handicap? Before a person can conquer a handicap, he must master his own feelings.

This isn't easy. Put yourself in the other fellow's place. You are in a bad automobile accident and wake up in a hospital, unable to move your legs. You are bound to feel mighty blue, especially when you learn that you will have to live with this handicap all your life. For weeks you lie on your back, feeling more and more sorry for yourself.

You feel helpless too. Nurses bathe you and turn you over in bed. You get used to this after a while and expect people to wait on you.

Then suddenly everything changes. You are at the Institute to be rehabilitated. People in wheel chairs are lifting dumbbells. Others are standing in their braces, doing crutch exercises. No one has time to feel sorry for you. Even the doctors don't seem to realize that you are too badly hurt to take exercises. Early next morning they expect you to slide out of your gown, into a T-shirt and slacks, and go to work.

What a day! First comes "stretching." You lie face down on a table with ten-pound weights hanging from your ankles. You hear your joints crackle. After an hour your eyeballs are ready to pop. Weight-lifting is next, and then you do push-ups on the mats. After lunch, there is more of the same. All this when you can't even sit up! You want to go home and be waited on in bed.

Like most new patients, Joseph R. Larsen felt this way at first. He turned to the man next to him in the gymnasium for sympathy.

"Tough luck, Mac," his companion told him. "You can only fight it so long. Once you pick up that weight, you're lost. Five pounds today, ten pounds tomorrow. They rehabilitate you in spite of yourself."

Sure enough, Mr. Larsen *was* rehabilitated, and later wrote about his experiences for the Institute's magazine. He can laugh now, but it wasn't funny at the time.

Monday morning, Charlie, the wheel chair man, came around.

"But I can't sit up," Mr. Larsen yelled. "Think of my bed sores."

"Don't worry, boy," replied Charlie. "Each chair

comes fully equipped with fur-lined cushion and a bottle of plasma."

On Tuesday it was John, the brace man. "Stand?" shouted the patient. "Yesterday I sat. Now I gotta stand. When are you guys going to realize I'm an invalid?"

Then there was ADL—short for "activities of daily living," such as getting into the bathtub.

"But I don't want a bath. I get bathed in bed," said Mr. Larsen.

"Now come, lad, we are getting rehabilitated, aren't we? Remember now, if you fall getting in, don't get out and try it again. Have your bath first, then get out and try it again."

Finally, Mr. Larsen took Dr. Rusk's advice. He decided to sign his own Declaration of Independence. At the Institute this means you make up your mind that you will learn how to take care of yourself and not go through life depending on others.

The doctors, physical therapists, occupational therapists, and nurses at the Institute are there to work *with* patients, not *on* them. A paraplegic who is determined to get out of his wheel chair learns to use a new set of muscles. Since his leg muscles no longer do what they are told, he cannot walk in the usual way. Instead, he lets his arms and shoulders do the work and "ambulates." Placing his crutches ahead of him, he "swings through" each step. At first he ambulates between parallel bars to keep from falling. Then come the first steps outside the bars. It takes long practice to learn how to balance without support.

"Raise the crutch just one more time," says the physical therapist—until finally the patient can stand erect, even though he has no feeling in his legs.

Patients also practice lifting themselves over make-believe curbstones so they can cross the city streets. They climb a set of stairs, four steps up and four steps down, many times a day. One of the hardest things is learning to fall and get up again. It takes real skill to break the fall properly, retrieve the crutches, and get back on one's feet.

Other skills must be learned too—getting out of bed, going to the bathroom, washing and dressing, and putting on leg braces. The Institute teaches seventy-two of these "activities of daily living." Patients with stiff fingers learn how to button their clothes with a gadget that has a wire loop at the end. The Institute has a roomful of these "self-help devices" for the handicapped. There are long-handled forks, spoons, and toothbrushes for people who can't raise their arms up high. Other utensils have straps or clasps to fit on fingers that don't grasp objects well. A magnetic writing board lets one-armed people write without the paper slipping around. Two little iron cubes hold the paper down, and the board does the rest. Another device turns the pages of a book. You lie in bed and work it with your feet.

The occupational-therapy workshop has tools and machines of various kinds. By making things, patients limber up their muscles and joints. "Maybe I really can earn my living again," they say.

Women who keep house are not forgotten either. There is a model kitchen which can be run from a wheel chair. The shelves, work counters, stove, ironing board—everything—are low and easy to reach. A woman on crutches can use this kitchen too. The counters have half moons cut into them and are equipped with belting. The housewife straps herself inside and works without crutches.

The swimming pool at the Institute is always popular. If you can't climb in, you can be hoisted in. Up you go, lying on a canvas stretcher, then down into the pool. Children at the Institute get swimming lessons as part of their school work. A former polio patient, if he has some muscle power left, may find that he can kick his legs again. The water bears his body up and makes motion easier.

Rehabilitation centers are starting up in many parts of the country. They have a big job to do. Experts say there are two million disabled Americans who could be taught to take care of themselves and make a living. They range from youngsters with cerebral palsy to old people partly crippled from arthritis. To meet the tremendous need, more and more doctors are receiving specialized training in physical medicine and rehabilitation. They need trained helpers too. Thousands of jobs are opening for physical therapists, occupational therapists, speech and hearing therapists, vocational counselors, special teachers, and social workers. Anyone who likes people a lot, and doesn't mind hard work too much, has a chance for a satisfying career in this new field.

11

doctors in the armed forces

When doctors go sightseeing in Washington, D.C., they visit the Army Medical Museum. It was started during the Civil War to illustrate the results of gunshot wounds. Surgeons on duty with the Union Army shipped the first specimens of wounded tissue in barrels of alcohol so that they would keep. The flesh wounds are preserved in jars of alcohol to this day. Shattered bones have been dried and mounted. Today the museum has a world-famous collection of war wounds. The earliest of these were produced by Indian tomahawks, the latest by atomic bombs.

Whenever men go into battle, there is important work for doctors to do. Even in peacetime, doctors in the armed forces keep busy. They treat the sick and injured and stand guard against influenza, measles, and other diseases that spread rapidly among men who live close together in barracks. Military doctors also know about sicknesses in other parts of the world. They vaccinate soldiers and sailors who are bound overseas against diseases they may meet in their travels such as typhoid fever, cholera, and yellow fever.

It was a group of army doctors, headed by Dr. Walter Reed, who proved that yellow fever is spread by the bites of infected mosquitoes. Their brave experiment was held in Cuba in 1901. During World War II, doctors in the armed forces won new victories over insect foes. One of their weapons was DDT, the new insect killer. They used it against lice that spread typhus and mosquitoes that carry the parasites of malaria.

More people have suffered from malaria, and died from it, than from any other disease in the world. In the tropics, where the battles of the Southwest Pacific were fought, doctors took it for granted that every wounded soldier also had malaria. Usually they were right. It was not possible to kill all the mosquitoes in that huge part of the world. The best medicine then known was quinine, and most of it was in the hands of the Japanese enemy. Chemists developed thousands of new compounds and sent the most promising of them to the armed forces. Army doctors tested the medicines on soldiers who were shaking with the violent chills of malaria. A few of the medicines were even better than quinine.

After the war, the fight against malaria continued. In January 1954, Surgeon-General George E. Armstrong of the United States Army told about "our victory over malaria" in an article in *The Military Surgeon*. Malaria is still an important military problem, he said, but two drugs, chloroquine and primaquine, now control the disease and kill the infection so well that malaria no longer puts troops out of combat.

The Civil War gunshot wounds that you can see in the Army Medical Museum killed about fourteen out of every hundred injured soldiers. The shell fragments, mortar fire, anti-aircraft flak, and booby traps of World War II were far more damaging to flesh and bones than gunshot. Yet only four out of one hundred of the wounded died. The record of the Korean War was even better. Out of every one hundred wounded soldiers reached for treatment, ninety-eight were saved.

The credit for this improvement belongs to the doctors of the armed forces and the nurses and corpsmen who served with them. They went where the fighting was, knew what to do, and did it quickly.

Medical corpsmen were with the troops as they went into battle. They gave first aid to the wounded and carried them on litters to battalion aid stations. Here doctors stopped the bleeding, put on dressings and splints, and gave drugs and blood plasma. Often the plasma was a real lifesaver. It filled out the volume of blood and kept the circulation from collapsing.

Jeeps and ambulances transported the wounded to

bigger stations a few miles back. From here, patients in no immediate danger moved on to evacuation hospitals. Those too critically injured to wait received immediate attention from surgical teams. Sometimes there was a mobile surgical hospital in a tent or a school within six or eight miles of the front. Ambulance helicopters went into action during the Korean War. They landed at the battalion aid station, picked up the most seriously injured, and took them directly to the mobile hospital.

Patients received whole blood of the right type and were prepared for emergency operations. X-rays located shell fragments and bone injuries. The operating room might have a dirt floor, but the team was complete with surgeons, assistants, anesthetist, and nurses. Surgeons always assume that any battle wound is contaminated with germs. So they cut away all dead tissue, leave the wound as clean as possible, and pack it with gauze. Later it is sewed up at a larger hospital, farther in the rear, after the surgeons can be sure that no germs are still inside making trouble.

In the old days, a soldier with a piercing wound of the abdomen had only a fifty-fifty chance of living. Germs rapidly invaded the body and were often beyond control when the patient reached the hospital. Now penicillin plus quick surgery saves most of these men.

Chest wounds used to be even more dangerous. Worst of all were "sucking" chest wounds, with air whistling in and out of a bullet hole with every breath. Soon the lung collapsed from the air pressing in on it. Today surgeons can open the chest and repair the damage while life-giving oxygen flows into the lungs under pressure.

During the Korean War, surgeons learned how to sew blood vessels together better than ever before. This is very important because almost two-thirds of all war wounds are injuries to the legs and arms. If too many blood vessels are put out of action, and not repaired, the tissue dies, and the limb has to come off. Today you don't see as many ex-soldiers with stumps as your parents did. Doctors save most of the arms and legs.

Even when a limb is lost, there are useful artificial ones to take its place. One is an arm with fingers that really work. The owner can pick up things, use tools, and hold a baseball bat. He moves the fingers with a chest muscle or one of his remaining arm muscles. The surgeon makes this possible by bringing a loop of muscle out into the open and grafting a covering of skin over it. A plastic hook fits into the loop and connects with the hand. The muscle, pulling on the hook, works the fingers. The hand looks lifelike and is covered with a cosmetic glove of the same tint as the owner's skin. These gloves were developed at the army's Walter Reed Medical Center in Washington.

Though most wounded soldiers return to their own outfits in a few weeks, those who need difficult operations can be flown quickly to the United States from any other part of the world.

Sometimes a soldier's wounds heal but he is left with bad scars or part of his face gone. Plastic surgeons work wonders in making him look like himself again.

A plastic surgeon is both an artist and a doctor. He is a sculptor who uses living tissue in place of wood or marble. He takes skin, bone, cartilage, even fat and muscle, from one part of the body and repairs defects in another part. Clear, smooth skin from the thigh, for example, covers a raw, grainy area on the shoulders where the skin has not healed well. Skin grafts must come from the patient's own body in order to "take." Grafts from other people are useful for covering bad injuries temporarily but they soon die. There is only one exception. A graft from an identical twin will work. However, people who aren't twins don't have to worry. If they are healthy, they can spare many grafts, for the skin soon grows back.

Sometimes ordinary grafts won't do. For a deep wound the surgeon needs both skin and the blood vessels that nourish the skin. In this case, he doesn't cut the graft completely off. He loosens a long flap of healthy skin, near the wound if possible, being careful to leave one end connected to the body so that it will receive a supply of blood. Then he swings the loose end around and sews it over the wound, using tiny stitches. Before long the skin is receiving blood from its new moorings, and the surgeon cuts the other end loose.

Sometimes the surgeon can't get the skin he needs near the wound. In that case he uses a "caterpillar flap." He "jumps" the flap from one part of the body to another by stages. Suppose he decides to move a flap from the abdomen to the neck, never letting it lose its blood supply. As soon as he raises the flap on the abdomen, he starts the loose end growing on the arm. When it is safely anchored there, he detaches the other end from the abdomen. Now he can raise the arm to the neck, tie it in place there, and sew down the flap over the neck injury. When once again it finds a new supply of blood, the surgeon cuts away the connection with the arm.

Plastic surgeons can make new lips with flaps from the scalp or chest. They build new chins from grafts of leg bone. They can construct a new nose. A flap from the forehead becomes the outside of the nose. Small flaps from the cheeks form the lining. Of course the nose needs some stiffeners inside or it will droop. For these, the surgeon takes some cartilage from the ribs, models it into pieces of the proper shape, and sets them in place.

Making a new nose is easy compared to some of the problems the armed forces are now asking doctors to solve. When a pilot cruises at an altitude of ten miles, or a submarine crew stays under water for weeks at a time, things happen to the human body that doctors have never had to deal with before.

Take the simple matter of breathing. It is no longer simple above fifteen thousand feet. The air becomes so thin that unless the pilot receives extra oxygen, he shows the results more and more as he climbs. Doctors who specialize in aviation medicine have studied these changes. The personality changes first. Air Force pilots are carefully selected for dependability and an even disposition, but at eighteen thousand feet some grow hilarious and others moody or quarrelsome. Their judgment becomes poor, like that of a drunken driver. They can no longer do problems in arithmetic. Dizziness sets in, the pilot's head aches, he has "butterflies in the stomach." At twenty thousand feet he passes out. All for lack of oxygen.

Air is about one-fifth oxygen. A pilot can increase this amount by breathing through a mask that is connected with a tank of oxygen. In this way he can fly up to thirty-five thousand or forty thousand feet. At that altitude he must breathe pure oxygen. Also he is likely to feel pains in his knee and finger joints. They are due to little bubbles of nitrogen leaving the tissues of the body as the pressure of the atmosphere grows less. At fifty thousand feet the pilot's lungs are so full of expanding carbon dioxide and water vapor that breathing soon becomes impossible.

To go higher still, one more thing can be done. Air can be forced into the cabin of the plane with a supercharger until the atmospheric pressure inside is like that on the ground. Then it is no trick at all to cruise eight or ten miles above the earth. Of course, the pressurized cabin might spring a leak, or in wartime enemy fire might crack it open. In that case, the crew would have a few seconds to get into oxygen masks. The oxygen would see them through until they lost altitude or bailed out. However, anyone who dawdled would topple over unconscious.

Doctors know this because they have tried it out in special pressure-chamber experiments at the School for Aviation and Space Medicine at Randolph Field in San Antonio, Texas. Fliers in training go through workouts in these chambers, where the pressure is like that at high altitudes, so that they will grow accustomed to the conditions they may meet.

It is the job of air force doctors to find out how people can live in the sky world and stay healthy. Teams of doctors and engineers are at work on pressurized suits for flyers. They are designing electrically heated clothing, oxygen cylinders for use while falling by parachute, and immersion suits to protect those who fall into the sea.

The g-suit is a special number for supersonic pilots. When a plane pulls out of a power dive, the blood rushes from the pilot's head toward his feet with several times the force of gravity. His eyes first feel the loss of blood. At 6g, or six times the force of gravity, he may black out and be unable to see. After that, he loses consciousness. The g-suit has pressure chambers around the stomach and ankles. They look like rubber bubbles and press the blood back when it rushes down. In this way the pilot can take more g's.

Navy doctors are learning how men can swim safely under water for a long time or at great depths. Underwater demolition teams of "frogmen" stay under water two hours. They can leave a submerged submarine under way and can go, accomplish their mission, and return safely to the submarine. In Operation Hideway, at New London, Connecticut, twenty-three navy volunteers stayed sealed up in a submarine for two months. The air they breathed had increasing amounts of carbon dioxide. Studying the results, the doctors learned new facts about how much punishment the body can take in new surroundings.

Submarine medicine—aviation medicine—and now, space medicine. Dr. Louis H. Bauer, former president of the American Medical Association, sometimes talks to other doctors about the horizons of space medicine. He points out that the space traveler will need protection against many dangers. He must pass through freezing cold in the upper atmosphere and frying temperatures higher up. He may have to travel in a capsule. He will need lead shielding too, thinks Dr. Bauer, because above seventy thousand feet he will be bombarded by heavy atomic nuclei. Higher still, the sun's ultraviolet rays are blistering and deadly. Up a hundred miles is a belt of meteorites. The space doctors of tomorrow have plenty of work ahead. But despite the difficulties, Dr. Bauer is hopeful. He believes that flights to the moon and finally to the other planets are perfectly possible.

12

doctors who guard public health

California is in the southwest corner of the United States, and San Diego is in the southwest corner of California. It is one of the fastest growing cities of the nation. Thousands of men work in the big airplane plants there. San Diego is a navy center too, and the streets are full of bluejackets from ships in the harbor. Elderly couples stroll through Balboa Park. They have come to San Diego to enjoy the sunny climate after a life of hard work. Plenty of young couples, too, are making their homes in this pleasant land. Twenty thousand babies are born in San Diego County every year.

New towns are springing up like magic around San Diego. You won't find them all on a map unless it is a very recent map. But the towns are there, with rows of white stucco houses, and gay flower beds, and playpens on the lawns for the babies. Busy shopping centers are opening up where lemon and orange trees grew a couple of years ago.

All this makes Dr. J. B. Askew a very busy man. He is Director of Public Health for the city and county of San Diego. It's his job to guard the health of all these people—old-timers and newcomers alike.

Helping the doctor is a team of public-health nurses, sanitary engineers, health educators, and other workers. There is never a time when all of them can sleep.

A milk-delivery truck is making its rounds at four in the morning. One of Dr. Askew's men stops the truck and gets a sample of milk to test at the public health laboratory. The Health Department watches over the milk carefully, from the dairy farm to the doorstep, making sure everything is sanitary.

Every highway leading into San Diego is lined with new trailer camps and motels where tourists can spend a night, a week, or a whole winter. Is the water safe to drink? Is the sewage disposed of safely? Do the gas heaters have vents so that no one will be in danger from the fumes? The health department finds out the answers before trouble happens.

It tests the city's water for purity every day. The water is also checked to see whether it contains the proper amount of fluorine—one part in a million. The water is fluoridated to protect the teeth of San Diego's children.

"Our children under ten years of age can look forward to only one-third the amount of tooth decay children have experienced in the past," says Dr. Askew.

San Diego has no city dump for rats to breed in. It doesn't burn its rubbish in smoky incinerators either. In California, smoke plus fog spell smog. And smog chokes people up, makes their eyes smart, and can even cause sinus trouble. Instead excavating machines dig deep holes out in the country, and the rubbish is buried.

If a dog bites the paper boy or the mailman, Dr. Askew hears about it in a hurry. It is necessary to watch the dog for signs of rabies so that the person who was bitten may be treated promptly.

San Diego's doctors call Dr. Askew's office whenever they see a case of any contagious disease. Then the Health Department tries to stop it from spreading.

If a man has tuberculosis, Health Department workers try to find out where he caught it. They arrange examinations for his wife and children to see whether he has passed on the disease to them. Anyone with tuberculosis is urged to get treatment at once. The sooner treatment begins, the more easily tuberculosis is cured. Often rest in a sanitarium is necessary. Sometimes the father of a large family says, "I can't afford to stop work. My children would go hungry."

"We won't let them go hungry," promises a social

worker from the Health Department. She arranges help for the family while the father is away getting well. .

The health department keeps a list of people with tuberculosis and watches the progress of every case. Dr. Askew doesn't wait for new cases to be reported but sends out the Chestmobile to look for them. The Chestmobile is a mobile trailer unit with an X-ray team in charge. It stops in a town, and everyone is invited to walk in and have a free chest X-ray. It visits the ranch country and X-rays the fruit pickers and cow hands. Back in the city, it calls at a factory. Not long ago more than twenty-three thousand San Diego aircraft workers had X-rays on the job. In any large group a few people always have early tuberculosis or other diseases and don't know it. They are lucky to find out while there is still time to prevent the condition from growing more serious.

Another way to prevent disease is to see that babies have the right start in life. Health Department doctors, nurses, and nutritionists hold more than six hundred Well Child Conferences in San Diego County every year. Mothers bring their babies and young children to these conferences for "shots" against diphtheria, tetanus, whooping cough, and smallpox. Each child has a physical checkup, and the mother receives answers to her questions about proper care and feeding.

Dr. Askew is also looking ahead to the health needs

of people at the other end of life. "San Diegans are living longer today than they did fifty years ago—in fact, almost twenty years longer," he says. "That is one reason why the chronic diseases such as heart disease, cancer, and diabetes are showing an increase in death rates. Many of these diseases can be discovered by simple tests in the early stages when they can more easily be cured or their harmful effects minimized." Health departments are becoming interested in the early discovery of *all* diseases—not just the contagious ones.

Everyone needs to know more about staying healthy and making his town a healthy place in which to live. So Dr. Askew's department carries health messages to the people of San Diego through posters, leaflets, newspaper articles, and radio and TV programs. Every day an average of five health films are shown in schools and community centers.

San Diego is becoming a health-conscious community, which is just what Dr. Askew wants it to be. "It is our job to protect the public health," he says, "but we can't do it alone."

Public health education is constantly changing our habits for the better.

Your grandfather may remember when people drank from the same cup in public places. The cup hung by a chain from the town pump or the faucet in the railroad station. Every time someone had a drink, he carried away other people's germs and left some of his own behind. Today we use paper cups or drinking fountains.

Some of your grandfather's schoolmates probably suffered from bone tuberculosis. Milk from sick cows caused this disease. Today dairy herds are tested for tuberculosis, and people drink pasteurized milk. As a result, bone tuberculosis is a rare disease.

Typhoid fever is rare too, because people use pasteurized milk and guard their drinking water against pollution.

People used to think it was just as natural for children to have lice as for dogs to have fleas. Skin diseases like scabies were common too. Then health departments began teaching the importance of cleanliness. Public-health nurses showed mothers how to wash their babies and keep sick people away from well people. Children playing on the streets of New York often saw the nurses from the Board of Health on their rounds. Little girls, bouncing a ball on the sidewalk, chanted the words of a new ditty. This is how it went:

> Marguerite, go wash your feet;
> The Board of Health's across the street.

Dr. Leona Baumgartner, who remembers this story, is now New York City's Commissioner of Health. She has watched many changes take place and has helped bring them about. In 1924, diphtheria took the lives of 714 of the city's children. Then came a big campaign to immunize every baby. In 1953 there was only one death from diphtheria in the nation's biggest city.

Health departments keep records of deaths and births so they can plan their work better. One baby out of ten used to die before its first birthday. Now few babies die, except some of the premature ones. But Dr. Baumgartner doesn't want "preemies" to die either. So she is a real booster for the Health Department's Premature Transport Service. This service has ambulances to rush premature babies to hospital centers for expert care. As the ambulance goes clanging past Times Square and Radio City, a nurse is riding inside with a tank of oxygen, helping the tiny patient make the trip in safety.

Sometimes a doctor wants to send a patient to the hospital for a number of examinations, but the patient cannot afford the expense. A New York doctor can send such a patient to the Health Department's Diagnostic Service Center, where the examinations will be made for nothing.

Nearly eight million people live in New York, and all of them live close to one of the Health Department's district health centers. These centers, with their classes and clinics and free health literature, are a big influence in teaching good health habits to the neighborhood.

Health departments inspect swimming pools, destroy ragweed before the hay-fever season, and guard the health of the public in many ways. Almost every city and town has a health department. Sometimes the health department serves the entire county, or even several counties if the population is small. Unfortunately, some out-of-the-way places have only a part-time doctor for this work, or even no health department at all.

Besides local health departments, there is a department of health in every state. It has experts who help the local public-health people with special problems, investigate outbreaks of disease, and do various laboratory tests for doctors and health departments throughout the state.

The United States Public Health Service in turn helps the states in many ways and defends our shores from invasion. The invaders that Uncle Sam's doctors worry about most are rats and mosquitoes. Rats carry fleas, and the fleas may be infected with the germs of plague, the dreaded Black Death. So if a ship comes from a port where there is plague, it doesn't dock until it is free of rats. Mosquitoes prefer airplane travel, so planes from yellow-fever regions get a careful going over for hitch-hiking insects. Government doctors have done outstanding work in tracking down the cause of many diseases and learning how to combat them.

Today most public-health doctors are specialists who have advanced training beyond medical school.

The interests of these doctors must be as wide as the ever-changing world. They have licked many problems, but there are always new ones. Take the problem of the wastes that are left over in plants that use radioactive materials. How are you going to get rid of atomic wastes? They can't be dumped into a river like other wastes. Swimmers would get atomic burns. The fish might become radioactive. If you bury atomic wastes, someone may dig them up by mistake. Some wastes stay radioactive for years or even centuries. How are you going to warn people to keep away when they are not even born yet? That is a real stickler for the public-health doctors of tomorrow.

13

doctors and mental health

Brave men are almost always afraid. They face danger in spite of fear. But they aren't "fearless." If a man had no fear to overcome, how could he be brave?

Army doctors talked to forty-five hundred fliers during World War II. Ninety-nine out of every hundred of these men admitted they were afraid. Perhaps the hundredth man was afraid to admit it!

The fliers told how it feels to be afraid. The heart speeds up, the mouth is dry, the hands are sweaty, the stomach feels uneasy.

"At first I was afraid of being a coward, of letting the rest of the crew down," said one flier. "Later on I got over that. It was enemy action I was afraid of then."

"What kind of enemy action bothered you the most?" asked a doctor.

"Anti-aircraft fire. We were helpless to do anything."

"How about fighter planes?"

"Not so bad. We could fight them back."

This was one of the things the doctors learned about fear in combat. Fear was easier to stand when you could do something about it. Another thing that helped was to know you were not alone. A flier gained courage from his buddies, his leaders, and his smooth-running equipment. During a mission over enemy territory, he kept busy at his job and joked over the interphone with the other crew members.

As time went on, the fliers felt tired and moody between trips. They lost their appetite. Loud noises made them jumpy. After thirty-five flights over Germany, even the best of these carefully picked men needed rest before starting another tour of combat duty.

The doctors who made this study of fear were psychiatrists. After the war some other psychiatrists watched a submarine crew that stayed under water for two months during Operation Hideout. The quarters were cramped, and there was little chance to "blow off steam." As the weeks went by, the men grew tense. Everyone had gripes. But not everyone showed irritation in the same way. Some "got it off their chest" without too much fuss and felt better. Some really "blew their tops." Some kept quiet but felt sulky inside. One man had to be babied. He complained about wanting cottage cheese and wouldn't stop until they gave him some.

People have various ways of acting when they feel angry or afraid. Some ways work better than other ways. Psychiatrists are doctors who learn all they can about people's feelings so they can help them live happier, healthier lives.

"Psyche" means mind, so psychiatrists might be called "mind doctors." Actually, emotions have so much to do with the workings of the mind that you could almost call psychiatrists "doctors of the emotions."

At one time, most psychiatrists worked in "asylums" or mental hospitals. They found out that so-called "crazy" people are much like the rest of us. They have the same emotions, only some of these emotions run to extremes. Everyone's emotions get out of hand now and then. Hardly anyone handles them as well as he might. An old Quaker once told his wife, "Everyone is a little queer except thee and me, and sometimes I have my doubts about thee."

So nowadays psychiatrists pay increasing attention to everyday emotional problems. Many colleges have a psychiatrist who advises students. Married couples who don't get along as well as they want to sometimes see psychiatrists. Some patients of psychiatrists are important business leaders or gifted television stars. These people, though successful, feel they are not making the most of their talents and could get more out of life if they learned better emotional control. Diagnostic clinics sometimes have a psychiatrist among their doctors. He talks to patients about any worries they may have just as other doctors record blood pressure or make X-rays.

Why do people worry? Psychiatrists say they worry because of anxiety. Anxiety is a kind of fear growing out of a person's inner feelings. It can be good or bad. If you are about to flunk algebra or lose your job because you are lazy, anxiety may help you buckle down to work. On the other hand, anxiety that goes on and on to no useful purpose is bad. People sometimes worry about a disease they will probably never get or feel guilty about something that doesn't really matter. Some people find it hard to relax and enjoy themselves on a holiday. They feel they are wasting time and should be working. They worry so much that they are worn out next day and can't do their best work. Lots of people worry without knowing the real reason. Psychiatrists help people get over useless anxieties like these.

About the most important thing in life is getting along with people. We all have our ways of doing this. Psychiatrists have found out some interesting facts about how we learn these ways. As babies, we howled when we wanted attention. It worked. As we grew older, howling didn't always get results. This was pretty hard to take. To show how we felt about it, we had temper tantrums. Or perhaps we were sorry for ourselves and sulked.

Some people stay like this all their lives and expect

to be babied. Almost anyone is likely to go back to this stage for a while if he suffers some great misfortune. As we know, people who become paralyzed have to fight two battles. The first and sometimes hardest battle is against self-pity. After that comes the battle against the physical handicap.

One thing that helps us grow up able to face life's problems is our parents' love. It makes up for the fact that we can't always have our own way. It teaches us to care about other people. It proves we are not alone in the world. The crowd we go around with teaches us more lessons. We grab someone else's baseball glove and get a poke in the nose. We fail to share a bag of candy and find ourselves unpopular. People of our own age teach us not to expect something for nothing. We have to respect the rights of others. And we don't like to be pushed around either. We stand up for our rights, but if we lose an argument or a fight, we don't go to pieces. Sometimes we have to compromise.

Poets have said that human beings are part animal and part angel. When we are very small, and someone makes us angry, we scream, "I'll kill you!" This is the animal part of us speaking. Soon we learn that killing people is something that isn't done. But we don't lose the animal side of our nature. For example, a man gets bawled out at work. He is afraid to talk back to the boss, so he comes home and takes it out on the family. He is cross with his wife, yells at the

children, and kicks the dog. Psychiatrists say it would
do him more good to dig in the garden or knock a
punching bag around.

Our animal nature, psychiatrists tell us, is nothing
to be ashamed of if we handle it right. In fact, it
supplies the energy we need to excel in sports, stick
to a goal with determination, and succeed in our life
work. Wrongly used, though, it can turn us into bit-
ter, unhappy people, envying others their achieve-
ments and hating those whose race or religion is
different from ours.

A noted psychiatrist says that the happiest and
most fortunate people in the world are those who
can give love to others and accept love from them.
By love he means not only love between parents and
children, or between husband and wife, but all the
friendly, helpful things people do for one another.

Liking other people helps us grow up emotionally.
One of our first loyalties is to our chums and our
"gang." We are part of the group. We belong. In
the teen years, we start dating, and before long we
feel at ease with the opposite sex. As we marry and
have children, we are devoted to our family. And if
we really like people, we have room in our hearts for
our friends and neighbors, the people we work with,
our community and our country, and our fellow men
everywhere. If a person is like this and also finds satisfaction in his work or hobbies, he is likely to be in
good mental health.

The National Association for Mental Health says that people in good mental health

> feel right about themselves
> feel right about other people
> are able to meet the demands of life

Of course, few people enjoy perfect mental health any more than perfect physical health. For that matter, doctors do not think of mind and body as two separate packages. They believe that a healthy mind makes for a healthy body, and vice versa. Doctors often say that half the common ills they see every day are partly due to emotional stress.

Here is an example of emotional stress. A man oversleeps, gobbles his breakfast, runs for the train, almost misses it, and reaches his office, where a big deal is on. His blood pressure is up and he hasn't digested his breakfast yet. If this happens too often, the man will be going to his doctor to say that he doesn't feel well.

"We can't be tense and react violently day after day to something we don't like without its doing things to us," says one doctor.

Almost all doctors, not just psychiatrists, are interested in mental health. This is good because there are not enough psychiatrists to treat all emotional problems. Besides, a person does not need to go to a psychiatrist for every worry any more than he goes to a surgeon for every stomach-ache. A wise family doctor or pediatrician understands that emotions get upset as well as stomachs. He has experience helping people and knows how to combine good psychology with his medicine.

Perhaps a high-school student feels depressed because he has failed to make the football team. He is afraid he will never be popular. But he has talent for music, and the doctor encourages him to become a good saxophone player. The student does so and finds that making friends comes easy after all. Another patient is a businessman. The doctor prescribes a "rest cure" because the man has worked himself into such a nervous state that he can no longer make good decisions. The next patient, however, needs a "work cure." He needs to face his problems and will feel better if he has something to do.

A woman feels lonely and unwanted. Her children have grown up, and she has nothing to do. The doctor knows that blind people need books in Braille which they can read by touch. "Why don't you give some of your time typing books for the blind?" he says. The woman accepts the suggestion. Being of use again does wonders for her health.

All medical students now study some psychiatry. Then those who want to specialize in psychiatry spend five years after medical school in advanced study.

People who go to a psychiatrist talk to him about their problems, and he helps them understand their emotions better. They tell him of experiences they have had at work, at home, or at school. Gradually they come to see why acting in certain ways always seems to get them into trouble. They learn new ways of using their emotions and try to make these new ways a real part of their lives. This kind of treatment is a sort of emotional re-education.

Sometimes patients have an "analysis." They discuss their life history very carefully with the psychiatrist. He is skilled in leading them back to long-hidden memories of the past which help explain their present way of acting. People sometimes have unreasonable fears, or feel guilty or depressed, or fly off the handle easily, and do not really know why. The purpose of the analysis is to make them understand how these feelings started. Then it is easier to build new and healthier emotional habits.

After terrible battle experiences, soldiers are sometimes unable to remember what happened. Yet they may feel deeply disturbed. Psychiatrists have found that they can give these patients an anesthetic by vein and, when the soldiers are half awake and half asleep, they are able to talk freely. Then the psychiatrist knows how to help them. Groups of soldiers have sometimes met together to talk over their problems under the leadership of a psychiatrist. Hearing that others have similar problems encourages them to face their own more resolutely.

Sometimes a psychiatrist works on a team with a

psychologist and a psychiatric social worker. The psychologist has many tests that help explain a patient's personality. One is a Rorschach, or an ink-blot, test. The patient tells what the ink-blot shapes look like to him and in doing so shows some of his inner feelings. The psychiatric social worker visits the patient's home and works with other members of the family so they too can help the patient get better.

About seven hundred thousand people are patients in mental hospitals. They occupy about half of all the hospital beds in the country. These people need care because they are too ill to look after themselves. Some are there because of brain damage due to disease, but most of them went through emotional storms that were too severe to bear. As a result, they took refuge in imaginary ideas.

Sometimes these people are called "insane," but this is a lawyer's word, not a doctor's word. An insane person is one who is mentally unfit to take responsibility for his acts, and in the past, insanity was often a tragic, hopeless state. But psychiatrists have now learned so much about various mental illnesses that a large proportion of patients are able to leave mental hospitals cured or greatly improved.

Patients at mental hospitals have many activities that help them gain a new interest in life. They play games, attend classes, and work in the garden. Music therapy, occupational therapy, and baths of various kinds may be part of the treatment. A new treatment by electric shock works wonders in many cases. The patient feels no pain but goes instantly into a sleep from which he awakens with a changed flow of thought.

Mental hospitals could be of even greater help to patients if they were not so crowded and if they had more psychiatrists and more trained psychiatric nurses and attendants. Many communities now have mental-health committees that are working for better conditions in mental hospitals. Another thing they are doing is to tell about the importance of mental health and to start psychiatric clinics where people can go for help before they are seriously ill.

In mental illness, as in all illness, prevention is better than cure.

14

beyond the call of duty

With average luck, a boy or girl born in the United States today will live to be about seventy years old—perhaps older, if doctors keep on making big discoveries. People who reach seventy have time to watch their children grow up, then their grandchildren. They may even become great-grandparents.

We enjoy so many advantages that it is easy to forget that the average length of life in Asia and Africa is only thirty years. Though many people live longer, many babies die before they are a year old.

In our own country, when George Washington was President, people lived an average of thirty-five years—only half as long as they do today. Also they were sick much more than we are. Washington was ill so much in his early years that he expected to die young. Once he was so sick that he rode into battle with a pillow in the saddle. This was at Braddock's Field during the French and Indian War. Young Washington's bravery on this occasion made him famous. And though he was never entirely well, he lived to be the "Father of His Country."

Today we have better food and healthier ways of living. Doctors have taught us the importance of these things. Sometimes they had to blaze trails through forests of ignorance. One of the most courageous pioneers was a woman. Her name was Elizabeth Blackwell.

Elizabeth was eleven years old when she sailed from England with her parents in 1831. It took many weeks to reach America. The steerage passengers in the hold of the ship ran out of food. Cholera broke out and added to their misery. Almost every day, bodies wrapped in sheets were buried at sea.

Elizabeth's tender feelings were aroused, but it did not occur to her that she could ever relieve such suffering as this. Girls never became doctors in those days. A doctor had to examine sick people and endure loathsome sights and smells. No nice girl, people thought, could possibly do this.

In school, Elizabeth was as finicky as the rest. One day the physiology teacher showed the class a jar containing the eye of a bull. It was fat and bloody inside. The sight made Elizabeth so ill that she went without supper and had bad dreams.

Later the Blackwell family moved west to Cincinnati. The country was changing. There were gas lights, free public schools, and railroads.

"What will they think of next?" people were saying. One of Elizabeth's friends was Mrs. Harriet

Beecher Stowe. She wanted to put an end to Negro slavery. Some women were even speaking up for the right to vote.

Elizabeth Blackwell was hardly grown when she lost her father. He died of a disease that doctors did not know how to cure. Later she watched the final illness of a woman friend of whom she was very fond.

"Why don't you become a doctor?" asked her dying friend. "A woman doctor would understand how women feel."

"Oh, I couldn't. I have always had a horror of the human body," replied Elizabeth.

Nevertheless, thoughts of being a doctor stayed in her mind. Surely she should do something worth while with her life. So many people needed help.

Elizabeth asked the family doctor's advice. He was shocked. "A woman doctor! Forget your foolish notion, my dear young lady, and learn to cook and sew instead," he urged.

Even the broad-minded Mrs. Stowe had doubts. "If you go ahead with your plans, you will fight a lone battle," she warned her young friend. But by now Elizabeth had made up her mind. She was going to be a doctor.

For five years she taught school. At night she studied medical books and came to see that the human body was not ugly, as she had supposed, but a thing of wonder and beauty.

Then Elizabeth went to Philadelphia, hoping to

enroll in one of the city's medical schools. But every school turned her down because she was a woman. After that she wrote letters to other medical schools all over the country.

The little Geneva Medical College in upstate New York finally accepted her. It was something of an accident. The decision was put to a vote of the students. In a spirit of horseplay they shouted, "Hurray for the lady student! Let her come!" However, Elizabeth Blackwell now had her chance. Her serious interest in medical studies soon won her the respect of teachers and students alike.

But it was still a lone battle in many ways. The ladies of the town turned their backs on Elizabeth. A little boy to whom she spoke cried out, "My mother says you are a bad woman," and ran away.

In 1849, Elizabeth Blackwell was graduated from medical school at the top of her class and became America's first woman doctor. After further study in Paris and London, she opened an office in New York. People on the street stared at the "lady doctor" and were surprised to see an attractive woman in a pretty dress. They had heard she wore trousers!

In all the growing city no one needed a doctor so much as the women and children of the slums. People who came to New York in search of work lived in dark, dirty tenements. Every ship from Europe brought in more people. Their ragged children got little air and sunshine indoors. Outdoors they played on garbage-littered streets.

Dr. Blackwell dreamed of a free dispensary where she could treat sick children and teach their mothers about cleanliness and good diet. Her zeal and the help of some good Quaker friends finally made the dream come true. Later the dispensary became the New York Infirmary for Women and Children, a great center for training women doctors and nurses.

For half a century Elizabeth Blackwell worked tirelessly, in the United States and in England too, as a doctor, medical teacher, writer, and lecturer. Schools for women doctors opened in both countries. More and more of the older medical schools accepted women students.

Elizabeth's sister Emily was one of those who followed in her footsteps and became a doctor. Emily told her, "You were first. It will never be so hard for me."

Today there are thousands of able women doctors. In almost any medical school you will see a number of girl students, hard at work beside the boys.

Dr. Blackwell died in 1910 at the age of eighty-nine. Carved on her tombstone are these words from her own writings:

"God's law for the human body is as sacred, nay, is one with God's law for the human soul."

Albert Schweitzer decided to become a doctor when he was thirty years old. His friends were astonished. It was late to take up a new profession.

Besides, Schweitzer was already launched on a brilliant career. He was principal of the theological college in Strassburg, a city which was then part of Germany; he was an able preacher and a gifted organist. He gave recitals of Bach's organ music in Europe's leading cities.

And now, at thirty, he was going to sacrifice his great talents and begin the long grind of medical school. That was not all. After he became a doctor he was going—of all places—to the jungles of French Equatorial Africa!

"It is the most unhealthy spot on earth," his friends told him. "Sleeping sickness, leprosy, malaria—every kind of scourge rages there."

"Then they need a doctor," replied Schweitzer.

"Others can go. You can do more good by preaching."

"I want to preach the religion of love with more than words. As a doctor I can work without having to talk."

"But your music!" they protested.

"I have found so much happiness in life that I must do something in return for it," said Schweitzer.

Six years later Schweitzer completed his medical examinations. After that, he studied tropical medicine in Paris and rounded up the equipment for a jungle hospital. In 1913 he set off for Africa. His wife, a nurse, went with him.

The journey ended at a mission station up the Ogowé River, which reaches the west coast of Af-

rica just below the Equator. Thick forests grew to
the river's edge and were mirrored in the water. It
was hot, rainy country. Crocodiles and hippopota-
muses swam in the river. The air swarmed with mosquitoes. Clouds of locusts and armies of traveler ants
made endless war on the little clearings where the
natives had their huts and garden patches.

The Schweitzers shared their jungle bungalow
with huge spiders and flying cockroaches. The doctor's first work place was an old henhouse which he
cleaned and whitewashed with his own hands. He
was the only doctor for hundreds of miles around.
Long before a hospital was ready, native canoes were
pulling up at the landing with patients for the doctor
to see.

One man whom friends carried up the hill was
moaning in pain. He had a dangerous kind of rupture known as strangulated hernia. Without an operation he would die in a few hours. Dr. Schweitzer
put him to sleep and repaired the rupture. The patient awoke free of pain and gazed into the doctor's
face. The two men could not speak each other's language but their eyes spoke for them.

This was Dr. Schweitzer's first operation. Before
long he had a better place in which to work—a cor-
rugated iron building with a roof of palm leaves.
Around it was a ring of bamboo huts for the patients.
Sometimes the little jungle hospital was swamped
with sick and dying people. During an epidemic of
dysentery, Dr. Schweitzer struggled to keep those

with the disease apart from the other patients. It was uphill work. How could you persuade a man who knew nothing of germs to stay away from a dying friend? If the man was from the same village, it seemed only neighborly to share a last meal with him, using the same dishes.

A destructive jungle sickness was elephantiasis. The skin grew so rough and the legs so swollen that they seemed to belong to an elephant, not a human being. This disease was caused by threadworms, one of many parasites which are man's enemies in tropical lands.

Another enemy was fear. People in the jungle lived in constant fear of wild animals, deadly snakes, and tsetse flies, whose bite caused sleeping sickness. They feared hunger, unseen evil spirits, and magic spells. Often their haunted minds cracked under the weight of so many fears. Dr. Schweitzer built an addition to his hospital for the mentally ill.

Certain tribes still practiced cannibalism. But the mission taught them better ways of life, and some of the doctor's most loyal helpers were former cannibals. When World War I broke out, his ex-cannibal friends could not understand why Europeans were killing one another. One of them told Dr. Schweitzer, "They must do it for cruelty alone, because I understand they do not eat the dead."

Dr. Schweitzer was from Alsace, which has changed hands between France and Germany in various wars. He spoke French and German equally well, but in the eyes of the law, at that time, he was German. So the French government took the Schweitzers away from the mission in Africa and held them as prisoners in France until the war was over. Then Alsace became French again. Dr. Schweitzer, now a French citizen, was free to return to Africa. But his health was broken and he spent some time getting well and raising money for his hospital. When finally he saw it again, the building was in ruins. The jungle had grown up to the doorway.

The doctor had to start all over again. He rebuilt his hospital and later built a new and larger one and trained many native workers to help him. Doctors and nurses from Europe also joined Dr. Schweitzer, and today the little hospital that began in a henhouse is an important center for promoting better health in French Equatorial Africa.

In 1952, after World War II, the aged Schweitzer was named for a Nobel prize. Other doctors had received Nobel awards for their medical discoveries. Dr. Schweitzer received his for advancing the cause of peace. He had spent a lifetime serving others, far from his homeland. He was a shining example of the spirit of peace on earth and good will toward men.

These are two stories of doctors who have gone beyond the call of duty to bring the benefits of medical science to the people of our land and of other lands. Many others might be told.

Since 1946 the World Health Organization has been working with the United Nations for "the attainment by all peoples of the highest possible level of health." More than seventy nations have joined hands through the World Health Organization to improve public health around the world. Doctors from many lands meet and map out campaigns against tuberculosis, malaria, yellow fever, leprosy, cholera, and plague. They develop plans to improve the health of mothers and babies.

As yet, many countries do not have enough trained public-health workers to carry on this vital work. The World Health Organization helps teach and prepare the people who are needed. It also searches for new and better ways of stopping the spread of disease.

One medical team went to Egypt to fight bilharziasis, a disease caused by worms that live inside snails. When a laborer walks barefoot in an irrigation ditch, the worms bore through the skin of his feet and get into his system. If an easy way to kill the snails is found, millions of people in many countries will be spared untold misery.

In Haiti, penicillin teams went from house to house, offering injections to people whose bodies were covered with the sores of a disease called yaws. The sores healed quickly. People talked about the good news on market days. The word spread from village to village, and the teams found a ready welcome wherever they went.

Now medical teams in tropical countries have a new, long-lasting penicillin that remains in the system as long as a month. Penicillin like this is a great convenience in out-of-the-way places where people sometimes travel a hundred miles to see a doctor and find it hard to get back again soon.

In southeast Asia, says the World Health Organization, there are a million villages without proper sewage disposal or safe drinking water. Many of the people also suffer from malnutrition, because they are too poor to buy enough food and know too little about a balanced diet.

Health education is needed all over the world. But some of it must be a special kind of education, for half the world's population still cannot read or write.

The United Nations Educational, Scientific and Cultural Organization has an exciting plan for "fundamental education." It believes that everybody needs to know how to stay healthy, be a good farmer or craftsman, lead a dignified home life, and have recreation. These are the fundamentals. But before they can be taught there must be teachers.

UNESCO (short for United Nations Educational, Scientific and Cultural Organization) opened its first school for teachers at Patzcuaro, Mexico, in 1951.

Dr. Luis Emilio Pinto of Colombia was there to represent the World Health Organization. Other teachers were experts in agriculture, home economics, and recreation. The students—nurses, teachers, sanitary engineers—were from all parts of Latin America. They worked in teams in Patzcuaro and twenty nearby villages, learning about fundamental education.

Patzcuaro was the Tarascan Indian capital before the time of Columbus. It stands by a large lake, and fishermen's nets are a familiar sight in the neighborhood. The people who don't fish raise corn, wheat, or beans, or make big Mexican hats called sombreros. Many of them are pure-blooded Tarascans, tall and proud. The young men are extraordinarily fond of basketball. Older men who can't read their own names can nevertheless read music and play an instrument in the village band. They are friendly people and welcomed the visitors from UNESCO, but they could hardly believe that strangers would come so far to help them.

At one village the UNESCO team helped build a basketball court and an open-air theater. After that, they weren't strangers any more. People listened to them when they talked about better wells and cleaner streets. Mothers who were feeding their young children on corn gruel learned to add other foods to the diet. As a result, children lived who would have died.

After a while, farmers around Patzcuaro were using steel plows instead of wooden ones. They fer-

tilized their fields and vaccinated their livestock
against disease. They put windows into their homes,
the family slept on beds instead of on mats, and the
pigs moved out of the house.

The people did not learn these things from books,
not at first anyway. The UNESCO teams taught the
first lessons with illustrated posters and films with
sound tracks. They helped the villagers make movies
and put on little plays. One play told about a man
who couldn't read. He gave the wrong medicine to
his child; he failed to heed a "Danger" sign; and he
got into all sorts of trouble. People began to see that
they needed to read in order to learn about health
and better farming. After that, they were willing
pupils.

Patzcuaro is only a beginning. Those who served
on the first UNESCO team are back in their own
countries, carrying on the work. Others have taken
their places at the training center in Mexico. New
centers are in the making in Africa, India, the Middle
East, and the Far East. They are designed to bring
more happiness and health to a billion human beings.

15

becoming a doctor

A doctor whose son wants to be a doctor is usually delighted. His son has chosen a fine profession. He can look forward to being of great help to others. He will enjoy the esteem of his fellow citizens and the satisfaction of work well done.

However, a doctor will tell his son—or anyone else's son—that it takes long, hard study to become a doctor. It means a life of heavy responsibilities. No one ought to set out to be a doctor unless his heart and soul are in the work.

A doctor does not finish school until he is about thirty years old. It adds up something like this:

	Years
Pre-school	6
Elementary school	6
Junior high school	3
Senior high school	3
College	4

	Years
Medical school	4
Hospital training	2 to 5
	28 to 31 years

Clearly, anyone who intends to be a doctor must be persevering and studious. More young men and women apply to medical schools than can be accepted. To have a reasonable chance of getting in, a student should be in the top third of his class at college, with especially good grades in chemistry, physics, and biology. He should have formed good study habits in high school and even earlier.

College students who plan on being doctors usually take a pre-medical course and call themselves "pre-meds." Much of their work is in the science laboratories. They have a year of physics and usually more than a year of chemistry and of biology. They also need a year of English and a year or more of a foreign language. Some medical schools require courses in mathematics, psychology, and the social sciences.

These "pre-med" courses can be finished in three years, and some students enter medical school at that time. Most pre-meds, however, spend four years in college. Several medical schools take only college graduates, and most medical-school deans think that four years of college is a good idea. It allows more time for literature, languages, history, social sciences, and perhaps art and music. A young person will make a better doctor if he knows something besides science and can talk to his patients about many things.

Pre-meds generally send applications to three, four, or five medical schools so that they will have a better chance of getting into one of them. They do this nearly a year in advance. Sometimes they try to get in after three years in college. Then, if unsuccessful, they try again a year later. Somewhat over half of all applicants are finally accepted.

While still in college, pre-meds take a Medical College Admission Test. It lasts about six hours and measures ability to read with understanding about various subjects, solve mathematical problems, and answer questions about science and modern society. The results help the medical school decide whether the student will make a good doctor. Also important are his college grades and letters of recommendation from his science teachers and perhaps his doctor.

The medical-school dean and a committee of professors spend many hours going over applications. Usually they ask an applicant to come to the school for a personal interview. "Why do you want to be a doctor?" is always one of the questions. Anybody who is looking for an easy living or glamour is sure to flunk this one.

Medical-school teachers want to know whether the applicant is a self-starter. They ask about his summer jobs and his interest in athletics or other student activities. Can he assume a responsibility and see it through? This is important because a doctor has to take positive action and make difficult, life-and-death decisions. He needs moral courage and calmness in time of emergency.

Does the applicant like people and understand them? A doctor cannot choose his patients as he does his personal friends. He must have sympathy and patience with all sorts of people and give his best efforts even to those who are unattractive and disagreeable. He needs to gain the confidence of his patients so that they will follow his advice. Above all, he must be honest. People stake their lives on what the doctor tells them.

Perhaps all this sounds as though only a superman could get into medical school. Actually, of course, no one is equally good in everything. A student with fine qualities of leadership might be accepted with some grades that are not quite tops. An applicant who does not mix readily with other people would find it hard to be at ease with patients. Still, if his scholarship is outstanding, he might be good in medical research or in some specialty in which other doctors send patients to him. Perhaps you have seen a doctor like this. People say, "He's not very sociable but he knows what he is doing."

All but two of the seventy-nine medical schools in the United States accept women students. A woman needs especially high qualifications, along with an interest in medicine that will continue if she marries and has a family. Throughout the country, about one medical student in sixteen is a woman.

A medical student needs good health. He faces long hours of study and after becoming a doctor must often work under pressure and with little sleep. Another thing a medical student needs is money. A medical education is expensive. By the time the four years at medical school are over, most students have spent about ten thousand dollars for living expenses, tuition, books, and microscope and other equipment. They need all their time for study and rest and can't hope to "work their way through" to any great extent. They can work during the summer and perhaps wait on tables or work in a hospital blood bank during the school year. Some get a little help from scholarships or student-loan funds. Certain states assist farm boys who promise to practice medicine in the country. Generally though, most of the money must come from the student's family.

Students who can't see their way through the long medical course might consider careers as medical technicians in hospital and research laboratories or as physical therapists, occupational therapists, or speech and hearing therapists. Medical and psychiatric social workers, pharmacists, dieticians, medical-records librarians, health educators, medical secretaries and assistants, and hospital personnel of many kinds are also needed. And there are many opportunities in nursing, even for men.

Medical students are usually about twenty-two years old when they enter medical school. Most likely their school is part of a university, but it may have a campus of its own several miles away or in another city. The location is often in a rundown neighborhood, even in the slums. This is a good place for a medical school, because a poor neighborhood has more patients who need medical care and cannot pay for it. A medical school looks like a big hospital rather than a college. In fact, some of the buildings *are* hospitals.

Before a medical student may work with patients, he must know the human body thoroughly. This is his big assignment for the first year. He has a thick anatomy book to learn from cover to cover. But he must know more than the book. He must know the body itself, how it looks and feels—every bone, organ, muscle, nerve, blood vessel, tendon, and gland. The only way to do this is by dissection.

Two, three, or four students team up and spend several months examining a human cadaver. The body is that of someone who died without home or friends. Now, in death, this person provides a way to help more fortunate human beings to have trained doctors. The work is not entirely strange to the students because they have dissected animal bodies in their biology labs at college. They are used to the smell, and soon they get used to the work and discuss it even at mealtime. It is part of the job.

First-year students study anatomy with the naked eye and under the microscope. They look at exhibits showing the development of the unborn child. As the year goes on they spend more time on physiology, studying the functions of the body, and on biochemistry, which is the body's living chemistry. They attend lectures in psychology and learn how the human personality changes through childhood, adult life, and old age. Perhaps once a week the professors wheel in patients whose troubles show why a doctor must know the workings of the human body.

During the second year, students learn to recognize the changes that take place in the body as a result of disease. In the pathology course they visit the hospital in small groups and watch their professor do an autopsy. This is an examination of the body of a person who has just died and is of great educational value to doctors. The appearance of the diseased organs shows the true causes of death more clearly than anything else can. An autopsy is performed as carefully as a surgical operation and leaves no marks that show at the burial. The dead person's family are usually willing to allow it to be done when they understand that it helps doctors to be of greater service to the living.

Second-year students prepare sections of diseased tissue for study under the microscope and on a projection screen. They learn about antibodies, bacteria, and the action of drugs upon the system. They become acquainted with various branches of medical practice through lectures and demonstrations. For the first time they examine patients on their own. They ask questions, write down the patient's medical history, and learn how to use the stethoscope, the blood-pressure apparatus, and their own five senses. Then they take blood and urine samples to the laboratory for tests and try to make a correct diagnosis. Of course the professor checks their work and points out any mistakes. Still, they begin to feel like doctors for the first time. Patients call them "Doctor." It is a grand feeling.

In the third year a medical student becomes a "clinical clerk" in a hospital. Now, after he makes an examination, he presents the patient to his professor at a teaching conference. He tells about the patient's past illnesses and symptoms. When the patient leaves, the class discusses the case. A clinical clerk goes with doctors on "ward rounds." They stop at the beds to see the patients and modify the treatment if necessary. It is interesting to watch the progress of patients from day to day.

Professors from various departments hold clinics and show patients with various diseases to the students. In some schools, a clinical clerk acts as a medical adviser to a few families. He makes home calls, finds out about health problems, and arranges for treatment. He learns to notice the connections between illness and the way people live.

In the third and fourth years, a student becomes acquainted with the different specialties—eye, ear, nose, and throat work, neurology, obstetrics, gynecology, pediatrics, and public health. He assists at operations and learns how to read X-rays, set fractures, put on casts and bandages, and perform minor surgery such as sewing up small wounds.

A fourth-year clinical clerk usually spends a great deal of time in the out-patient clinics where patients come for treatment. Here he sees the common complaints he will later treat in his own office. He still can't treat patients except under close supervision, but he finds out what it means to go through a busy day, helping dozens of people with minor ailments and trying to spot those who need special attention before real trouble starts. He also delivers babies and works with psychiatric patients.

Finally comes graduation and the solemn occasion when students repeat the Hippocratic Oath, as doctors have done for more than two thousand years. This oath is credited to Hippocrates, the Father of Medicine in ancient Greece. The student who is about to become a doctor promises to honor his teachers and to help teach others. "With purity and with holiness I will pass my life and practice my art. Into whatsoever houses I enter, I will go into them for the benefit of the sick. Whatever I see or hear, in the life of men, which ought not to be spoken of abroad, I will not divulge," he swears.

Now, at last the student is a Doctor of Medicine and may place the proud letters, M.D., after his name. Before he practices medicine by himself, however, he will spend at least one year, and probably two or more, in graduate study at a hospital. Sometimes this is the same hospital in which he worked as a student. Or it may be in a hospital in a town where he hopes to practice or one with specialists under whom he would like to study.

For a year the young doctor is an intern. He lives in the hospital, works long hours, and is called out of bed when a doctor is needed at once. He still works under the supervision of older doctors but is trusted to give various treatments and to know what to do in an emergency. He is the first doctor to treat most accident cases. He sees a good many babies into the world.

The intern is about twenty-six years old and would like a family of his own. But his earnings are small, perhaps seventy-five dollars a month, and he must wait to marry unless his family helps him or his wife works.

To make up for these sacrifices, the intern learns a great deal. On ward rounds and at clinics he presents cases to the older doctors. He watches over the medical students. In the "journal club" he reports on new articles in medical journals. He learns to think on his feet.

The intern also learns to be a medical detective. He goes to clinical-pathological conferences and matches wits with doctors of long experience. The procedure in clinical-pathological conference is like that in solving a difficult puzzle. First a doctor presents the case of someone who has died in the hospital. He tells about the physical examination, the laboratory tests, and what happened during the final sickness. But he holds back the diagnosis.

From what disease did the patient die? It *could* be one of several. The conference leader writes these on a blackboard. Then a doctor speaks up and says it couldn't be such-and-such because then one of the tests would have turned out differently. So the leader crosses off this possible diagnosis. One by one, others are eliminated until perhaps only a couple are left. The doctors discuss which diagnosis is most likely. This procedure is called "making a differential diagnosis."

Now comes a moment of suspense. Is the diagnosis right? The pathologist rises to his feet. He shows colored slides on a screen and describes his findings at the autopsy. These may show that the doctors were wholly right. Or perhaps they were largely right but missed some complication in the disease. Perhaps there is some hidden condition that is almost impossible to discover in a living person. Whatever the results, the intern sees clearly why a doctor must not jump to conclusions. He must pay heed to the tiniest clue.

Before applying for a license to practice medicine in his state, a doctor must pass the examinations that have been set up by a board of doctors. These examinations are required in order to maintain high standards of medical practice.

Sometimes a young doctor starts practice on his own after serving a year as an intern. There is so much to learn, however, that often he takes another year of training before setting up as a family doctor. If he intends to be an internist, a surgeon, or a specialist of any kind, he studies two, three, or four additional years and then takes a difficult examination in his specialty.

During these years of advanced study, he is a resident. He assumes increasing responsibilities for the care of patients and the training of younger doctors. He may become tremendously interested in some disease or scientific problem and do advanced work at a medical center for a year or two. Some doctors make a lifelong career of research or become medical teachers.

But whether a doctor does research, or teaches, or treats patients, he never really finishes school. Suppose a doctor had shut his books in 1940 and said, "I have nothing more to learn." Today he wouldn't even know about penicillin! So doctors keep on studying. They read medical journals and attend meetings to hear about new developments. They get together at the hospital and in their local and state medical societies, the American Medical Association, and various organizations of specialists. They attend clinics held by visiting doctors and take off a few days now and then for a postgraduate session in the big city.

A doctor who starts practice at thirty years of age may be thirty-five or forty before he has a good income. Even then, few doctors get rich. The average doctor today earns about fifteen thousand dollars a year—after he has worked many years for little or nothing. Still, he is proud of his profession. He can send his children to college. And if they want to be doctors, he can afford to send them to medical school.

Some doctors retire at the age of sixty-five but many remain active and vigorous until they are seventy-five or older. Being a doctor means a life of hard work, but a satisfying one.

16

what will doctors do next?

Doctors perform such astonishing feats that you wonder what they will come up with next. One of the best things they have learned to do is to change sickly "blue babies" into healthy ones. A baby whose heart pumps blood without much oxygen in it is bound to look blue. The blood isn't red, as it should be, but bluish, and shows up that way through the skin.

Dr. Helen B. Taussig of Johns Hopkins Hospital in Baltimore knew that blue babies are sometimes born with faulty hearts. Blue blood in the right side of the heart mixes with the scanty supply of red blood that comes to the left side from the lungs. The heart pumps out this weak mixture to the body. The tissues starve for oxygen. No wonder mothers told Dr. Taussig that their babies didn't grow like other children and were tired all the time.

How could more blood be sent to the lungs for oxygen? Dr. Taussig reasoned that vessels outside the heart might be made to do some of the heart's work. But she was not a surgeon, so she discussed her idea with Dr. Alfred Blalock, the hospital's chief surgeon. Together they figured out a way to shunt blood from one large artery into another artery that leads to the lungs. In this way, more blood passes through the lungs and picks up ogygen. Dr. Blalock has performed many "blue-baby operations" by linking the two vessels according to this plan. Other surgeons have learned how to do it too. It has changed hundreds of thin, weak children into rosy-cheeked youngsters who can run and play.

At Children's Hospital in Boston, Dr. Robert Gross performed other remarkable operations on the great vessels near the heart. Sometimes he repaired the main artery leading out from the heart with grafts taken from persons who had been killed in accidents. Today many medical centers have "artery banks," where the grafts stay in a deep freeze until needed.

Three Philadelphia doctors, in 1949, began operating on the *inside* of the heart. They repaired heart valves that were so badly damaged by disease that blood could barely trickle through. The surgeon cut a hole in the wall of the heart and pushed his gloved finger inside. Attached to the glove was a tiny knife with which he widened the valve opening.

This was an amazing but bloody operation, for all the time the heart was pumping away. The surgeon had to work quickly. Then, in 1952, a "mechanical heart" was used in an operation for the first time. The scene was Harper Hospital in Detroit. The patient was a factory worker with a leaky heart valve. On the operating-room team, in addition to the doctors and nurses, were two engineers in masks and gowns. They were there to run the mechanical heart. It was about the size and shape of an automobile engine and made of stainless steel, glass, and rubber. Inside were a dozen pumps.

Dr. Forest D. Dodrill, the surgeon, opened the patient's chest and clamped off the vessels that carry blood into and out of the left side of the heart. Working with him was Dr. Edward Hill, a plastic surgeon. Dr. Robert A. Gerisch, an internist, watched instruments that showed every change in the patient's condition.

The surgeon inserted a glass tube into each of the two blood vessels. Rubber tubing connected these glass tubes with the mechanical heart. Into the machine went some donated blood to start the pumps working. Next the clamps were removed. Blood from the lungs filled the glass and rubber tubing, flowed through the mechanical heart, and returned to the patient at a point beyond his heart. Then it circulated through the body until it reached the lungs again. The right side of the heart kept on working through the operation, but the mechanical heart did the work of the left side. The surgeons repaired the leaky valve in what they called a "dry field"—with no blood in their way. After they finished, the engineers reduced the pressure on the pumps, and the left side of the heart went back to work.

The operation lasted six hours. When the patient left the hospital, he felt better than he had for years.

In 1954, at the University of Minnesota Medical School, Dr. Clarence Lillehei's surgical team sewed up an opening between the two sides of a baby's heart. Instead of a mechanical heart, they used the baby's father. Father and child lay side by side on two operating tables. During the operation, a tube carried blood from the father's leg into an artery in his little son's chest. After flowing through the baby's body, the blood returned to the father. His heart and lungs did the work for both. Since then, other fathers have served as "mechanical hearts" for their children.

A surgeon who operates on a baby's heart for the first time wants to have a sure hand. Before he attempts the operation, he does a similar operation many times on dogs. The animal is under anesthesia and feels no pain, and the surgeon works as carefully as he would on a human patient. We owe a great deal to animals—not only dogs, but rabbits, guinea pigs, and the white mice and rats in medical laboratories. No new "wonder drug" is safe to take until it has been tested many times on animals. In fact, animals have played an important part in every kind of medical advance. At the same time, they receive much in return, for medical research helps cure animal as well as human diseases. Whenever the veterinarian gives a dog a "shot," he is using knowledge that came from studies with other animals.

Medical discoveries usually begin with the pioneer work of a medical team. Often the doctors are on the staff of a big medical center and teach at a medical school. A good way to see what doctors may be doing tomorrow is to find out what pioneer doctors at medical centers are doing today. Here are examples of interesting work under way.

Blood-fractionation machine: Blood from a donor flows into a centrifuge—a machine something like a cream separator. The machine draws out the plasma and separates red cells from white cells. By chemical means it takes apart the "fractions" of the plasma, such as those that give partial protection against measles and polio, or are useful in transfusions, or help clot the blood.

Eye banks: People sometimes sign papers giving a doctor permission to use their eyes after death. The eyes are placed in special containers and flown to an eye bank in a large city. Eye surgeons "draw" on this bank when they need a piece of cornea, or transparent eyeball coating, to take the place of eye tissue that is scarred or cloudy. It is like putting in a clear window in place of a frosted one and has restored sight in certain kinds of blindness.

Mosquito loudspeaker: Doctors have made recordings of the calls of disease-bearing mosquitoes. When they want to rid a district of mosquitoes, they set up cages with loudspeakers inside. The speakers send out the calls, and mosquitoes for miles around fly into the cages and are electrocuted. One call is the love call. This brings in the males. Another call means, "I've found blood," and attracts the females.

New drugs: By taking certain drugs under a doctor's direction, patients with epilepsy can do much to avoid having convulsions. Other new drugs are being tried out for the purpose of reducing the blood pressure when it becomes too high. There are even drugs for treating certain kinds of mental illness.

Electron microscope: Using a beam of electrons instead of light, it magnifies up to two hundred thousand times. For the first time, doctors know about the size and shape of viruses. Polio viruses are like little round dots. Perhaps twenty-five million of them could occupy the space on the head of a pin, says the National Foundation for Infantile Paralysis. Viruses are so much smaller than bacteria that it is like comparing the period at the end of this sentence with a circle drawn around a dime or a nickel.

Doctors want to do more than look at viruses. They want to know how viruses grow and spread disease and what they *are.* Are viruses chemical compounds or living creatures? Doctors are inclined to believe that viruses are alive, but are a very simple form of life. They multiply only in the cells of other living things. Our bodies make antibodies as a defense against some viruses. When doctors examine the blood of young adults, they find polio antibodies four times out of five. Most of these people say, "I never had polio," yet they must have had a mild case or the antibodies wouldn't be there. A new polio vaccine contains dead viruses which will produce these protecting antibodies early in life.

For protection against the influenza virus, we sometimes get "flu shots," only we have to have them every year. Probably you have heard people with flu say, "I've got that bug that's going around." By "bug" they mean the flu virus. Where do you suppose the "bug" stays when it is not going around? Doctors would like to know. A few years ago Dr. Richard E. Shope of the Rockefeller Institute for Medical Research *did* solve the mystery of one flu virus—the kind that causes influenza in hogs every fall. First, a hungry hog eats a juicy earthworm. Inside the earthworm are tiny lungworms, and inside the lungworms are viruses. The viruses wait until cold weather sets in, then flare up and give the hog the flu. That's not all. Lungworm eggs pass from the hog into the ground and are eaten by earthworms. Next year's crop of hogs will feast on these earthworms and complete the cycle. And all the time, the flu virus is hitch-hiking a ride!

It will be a big day for doctors when they discover the life story of viruses that cause human influenza.

Even more mysterious are the viruses of the common cold. In England, Dr. Christopher H. Andrewes has been trying to find out how people catch cold. He invites healthy young people to spend a free ten-day vacation in the country and act as "human guinea pigs." The volunteers stay in huts where they can't catch other people's colds. No one sees them except a masked and gowned doctor, who pours a few drops into their noses. Some of the volunteers catch cold and some don't, but either way they help the doctor learn more about colds. Dr. Andrewes has found that not all colds are caused by the same virus. He can "grow" colds outside the body in test tubes. Some day, he believes, doctors may know how to treat people's noses and throats so that they will make their own antibodies against colds.

The biggest medical hunt of all time is on in the campaign against cancer. Cancer is a wild growth of abnormal cells which is responsible for one death in every seven. Doctors who study cancer are searching out the innermost secrets of living cells.

Doctors have discovered hundreds of ways in which cancer starts in mice and rats—various chemicals, skin irritations, even certain viruses. It is good to have this information, but doctors are far from satisfied. There is a big gap between knowing what *can* cause cancer in a mouse and what ordinarily *does* cause cancer in a man. Hundreds of doctors at cancer-research centers are trying to fill in this gap in our knowledge.

Fortunately, cancer can be cured by surgery or X-rays if it is discovered early. Often, though, people do not learn they have cancer until so late that it is hard to do more than slow down its progress. Many cancers start in areas where it takes special tests to reveal their presence. That is one reason why doctors urge people to have frequent physical examinations, especially after they reach the middle years of life when cancer is more common.

If cancer could be detected as easily as tuberculosis, thousands of lives would be saved every year. For this reason, doctors are searching for a simple test of early cancer.

Meanwhile, they have high hopes that before too long even advanced cancer will be more successfully treated. Massachusetts General Hospital has a two-million volt X-ray machine. Hartford Hospital has an eight-ton "Theratron" which uses radioactive cobalt to destroy cancer cells. At the University of Chicago, Dr. Charles B. Huggins has added many years to the lives of certain cancer patients by changing the balance of hormones in their bodies.

Dr. Cornelius P. Rhoads, director of the Sloan-Kettering Institute for Cancer Research in New York, believes that the conquest of cancer may come largely through chemistry. Several drugs now being tested appear to act against cancer cells without harming normal cells.

Doctors are trying atomic medicine for some types of cancer. They give radioactive iodine for cancer of the thyroid gland. The iodine settles in the gland and gives off radiation which damages the cancer cells. Radioactive phosphorus attacks leukemia, or cancer of the blood-forming organs. Doctors plant radioactive gold deep inside the body in cancer growths that are hard to reach by X-rays.

Dr. Edward L. Bortz of the University of Pennsylvania School of Medicine recently told the World Medical Association that radioactive elements will prove as important for medical progress as the microscope. Doctors can "tag" foods, drugs, and hormones with small amounts of radioactive substances and trace their action in the body with instruments that pick up radiation.

"The use of radioactive tracers may completely revolutionize current understanding of body function, growth, and development," Dr. Bortz said. "Never before in the history of science has there been an inviting field of such promise for gaining clearer insight into the mechanics by which human life is sustained."

Doctors who explore the frontiers of atomic medicine have to be extremely careful. Isotopes—the radioactive forms of chemical elements—are "hot stuff." When a doctor receives a shipment from the atomic plant at Oak Ridge, Tennessee, he doesn't open it like a crate of oranges. Standing well back, he pries off the lead cover and tests it with a Geiger counter for any escaping radiation. In handling isotopes, he uses tongs or remote-control apparatus and works from behind a thick lead barrier. He never eats or smokes around isotopes. If any active substance were on his fingers, it could get into his system and settle down in some organ for days, weeks, or years.

Patients who are receiving atomic medicine may be "hot" too. Hospitals that use radioactive gold place a tag on the patient's bed warning other people to stay five feet away. A nurse may give back rubs and other treatments twenty minutes a day, no more. And she can care for only one radioactive patient.

Doctors use the findings of science, engineering, electronics and other branches of knowledge to find better ways of helping patients. The reason they know so much is that they are curious about everything.

Dr. Eugene Geiling of the University of Chicago wanted to study how digitalis, the heart stimulant, works. So he grew some radioactive lettuce and fed it to roaches. This made the roaches radioactive, and he fed them to tropical toads from Jamaica. From the toads he obtained a milky radioactive substance that mixed well with digitalis and acted as a tracer.

Dr. Otto Weininger of the University of Toronto knew that babies seemed healthier and happier when they got plenty of loving. He wondered how baby rats would respond. So for three months he cuddled and "gentled" a litter of recently weaned white rats. His little pets gained more weight and had stronger hearts, stomachs, and glands than rats that went without love. They were friskier, too.

Without curiosity there would be no medical research. Some of our most talented doctors spend their lives patiently learning how the body works in health and disease. They could earn more money in private practice, but they would rather do with less and satisfy their curiosity. When the late Dr. Walter B. Cannon was doing brilliant research at Harvard University, a successful surgeon asked him what he would do if he had all the money he wanted.

Dr. Cannon replied, "I *have* all the money I want. My wife gives me ten dollars a month and with that I pay my carfare, buy my lunches, and get my hair cut."

Medical research is carried on at medical schools and centers, at research institutes, by foundations, health organizations, and drug manufacturers, and at the National Institutes of Health at Bethesda, Maryland, near the nation's capital. These National Institutes are part of the Public Health Service of the United States Government and receive money from Congress for medical investigation. We Americans spend a fifth of a billion dollars yearly, all told, on medical research. That sounds like a lot of money, but it is a small amount compared to what we spend for candy, tobacco, or cosmetics.

If we supported medical research more generously, doctors could make even faster progress against cancer. They could learn many new facts about diseases of the heart, blood vessels, and kidneys, which cause more than half of all deaths. They could be of more help to the millions of people who suffer from some form of mental illness. Doctors would soon know how to prevent much of this mental illness. Perhaps they would find a cure for arthritis and rheumatism, which cause ten million Americans to be partly disabled. Much more needs to be known about some of the causes of blindness. The same is true of multiple sclerosis and muscular dystrophy.

Doctors have added years to our life. Now, as one doctor put it, they would like to "add life to our years" by making us healthier and happier in those extra years.

One doctor has figured out that increased medical knowledge has saved the lives of a million Americans in just ten years. All this is the result of yesterday's research. And tomorrow, we are sure, the record will be even more encouraging.

words doctors use

ALLERGY   sensitivity to certain substances, such as pollen, feathers, dyes, certain foods, etc.

AMBULATORY PATIENT   one who can walk around

ANATOMY   the structure of the human body or its parts

ANESTHETIC   a drug or a gas which produces a partial or total loss of conscious feeling or sensation

ANTIBIOTIC   a substance extracted from living organisms which acts against infections produced by other organisms

ANTIBODIES   substances produced in the body which fight invading germs and viruses

ARTIFICIAL RESPIRATION   the forcing of air in and out of the lungs by pressure or by a machine called a Pulmotor

BIOCHEMISTRY   the branch of chemistry which deals with the chemicals of the human body

BLOOD PRESSURE   the pressure of the blood against the walls of the blood vessels

BLUE BABY   a baby with a faulty heart which pumps a mixture of veinous and arterial blood. This results in an oxygen deficiency and gives the skin a bluish tinge

BRAILLE   a system of printing for blind people in which the characters are represented by raised dots

BRONCHOSCOPE   an instrument used for examining the inside of the windpipe and bronchis

CADAVER   the body of someone who has died

CAPILLARIES   the smallest blood vessels

CARTILAGE   the white, elastic substance which is attached to the surface of jointed bones. Sometimes called gristle.

CAST   a stiff bandage saturated with plaster of Paris or any other material which hardens when it is dry

CELL   any one of the tiny masses which make up organized tissue

CEREBRAL   having to do with the brain

CHRONIC DISEASE   one which continues for a long time

CIRCULATION   the movement of the blood from the heart through the body and back to the heart again

CLINIC   a place where several doctors work together

COMA   a loss of consciousness from which a patient cannot be aroused by stimulants

CONTAGIOUS DISEASE   one which is passed readily from one person to another

COSMETIC   something which beautifies the skin

DELIVERY ROOM   the room in a hospital where babies are born

DIAGNOSIS   the act of recognizing a disease by its symptoms

DISPENSARY   a place where drugs and medicines are prepared and distributed. Also a place where people who cannot afford to pay for them may come for medical or dental care and medicines

DISSECT   to cut apart

DRUG   any substance used as a medicine

ELECTROCARDIOGRAPH   a machine which electrically records the heart beats

FLUOROSCOPE   a machine for examining the inside of the body by means of X-rays

GAMMA GLOBULIN   that part of the blood which has many

antibodies to fight disease

GLAND   an organ which secretes substances to be used in or eliminated from the body

GRAFT   skin or other tissue to be joined to other skin or tissue

HEMOGLOBIN   the red pigment of the red blood corpuscles which carries oxygen

HORMONE   a chemical substance secreted into the body fluids by a gland, and which influences the activities of other organs

IMMUNE   protected against any particular disease

INTERN   a young doctor who is receiving advanced training under older doctors in a hospital

ISOLETTE   a glass-enclosed crib in which premature babies are kept

METABOLISM   the way in which the body makes use of food to build living tissue, and the way in which living cells are broken down

NUTRITION   the process of assimilating food

OCCUPATIONAL THERAPY   the treatment of disease or injury by work

OPHTHALMOSCOPE   an instrument for examining the inside of the eye

OUT-PATIENT   one who comes to the hospital for treatment but who does not have to stay there

PARAPLEGIC   someone who is paralyzed below the waist

PATHOLOGY   the branch of medicine which deals with structural changes of the body caused by disease

PHARMACY   a drugstore

PHYSICAL THERAPY treatment of disease by physical and mechanical means such as massage and electricity

PLASMA the liquid part of the blood

PLASTIC SURGERY surgery which restores tissues or lost parts of the body

PREMATURE BABY one born too soon

PSYCHIATRIST a doctor who treats disorders of the mind

RADIOGRAPH an X-ray picture

RASH a skin eruption

REHABILITATION the restoration of mentally or physically handicapped people to normal life

RESIDENT DOCTOR a doctor who is continuing his training from internship to a specialty

RETRACTOR an instrument for drawing back the edges of a wound

SANITARIUM a place where patients suffering from mental or physical diseases go for rest and treatment

SPECULUM an instrument used to open a body passage or cavity so that the doctor can examine it

STETHOSCOPE an instrument by which the doctor can listen to sounds inside the body, such as the heart beat or the air going in and out of the lungs

THERAPY the treatment of disease

TONGUE DEPRESSOR a small, flat wooden stick used to hold the tongue down while the doctor is making an examination of the throat or mouth

VACCINE material prepared from living organisms which can be injected into the body to make a person immune to a specific disease by forming antibodies

medical specialties

ALLERGY that branch of medicine dealing with allergy—
unusual sensitivity to certain substances which are
harmless to most people

ANESTHESIOLOGY the art and science of administering local
and general anesthetics to produce various types of
anesthesia

CARDIOVASCULAR DISEASE the diagnosis and treatment of diseases of the heart and blood vessels

DERMATOLOGY the science of the skin, its function, and its
diseases

GASTROENTEROLOGY the study of the stomach, the intestines,
and their diseases

INTERNAL MEDICINE that branch of medicine which is di-
rected primarily toward the diagnosis of symptoms

MALIGNANT DISEASES the treatment of diseases which are
more serious than the usual, because they tend to become progressively worse

NEUROLOGY that branch of medicine which deals with the
nervous system and its diseases

OBSTETRICS-GYNECOLOGY *obstetrics* is the branch of surgery
which deals with the management of pregnancy and
labor; *gynecology* is the branch of medicine which
deals with women's diseases

OPHTHALMOLOGY the branch of medicine which deals with
the eye and its diseases

ORTHOPEDIC SURGERY that branch of surgery which is concerned with the correction or prevention of deformities

OTOLARYNGOLOGY   that branch of medicine which deals with diseases of the ear and larynx

PATHOLOGY   the science which deals with the nature of disease—its causes and the changes produced in the body by it

PEDIATRICS   the branch of medicine which deals with children's diseases

PLASTIC SURGERY   surgery which is concerned with the restoration of lost, injured, and deformed parts of the body

PREVENTIVE MEDICINE   that branch of medicine which is concerned with preventing disease

PROCTOLOGY   the branch of medicine dealing with the rectum and its diseases

PSYCHIATRY   the branch of medicine which deals with disorders of the mind

PULMONARY DISEASES   that branch of medicine which deals with diseases of the lungs

RADIOLOGY   the branch of medicine which deals with radioactive substances and X-rays, and their application in the diagnosis and treatment of disease

SURGERY   the branch of medicine which treats diseases by manual and operative procedures

THORACIC SURGERY   the branch of surgery which is concerned with diseases of the chest

UROLOGY   that branch of medicine which deals with diseases of the genito-urinary tract

index